JOHN F. HAUGHT

D0060746

The Cosmic Adventure

Science, Religion and the Quest for Purpose

REGIS COLLEGE LIBRARY
100 Wellesley Street West
Toronto, Ontario
Canada M5S 2Z5

BL
240
.2
H38

REGIS COLLEGE
TORONTO
LIBRARY

PAULIST PRESS NEW YORK/RAMSEY

91561

Permission to quote material from the following sources is gratefully acknowledged:

A New Science of Life by Rupert Sheldrake. Copyright © 1981 by Rupert Sheldrake. Reprinted by permission of J.P. Tarcher, Inc., and Houghton Mifflin Company.
Reflections and Perspectives: Essays in Philosophy by E.D. Klemke. Copyright © 1974 by Mouton Publishers.
When Bad Things Happen to Good People by Harold Kushner.
Copyright © 1981 by Schocken Books.

Copyright © 1984
by John F. Haught

All rights reserved. No part of this book may be reproduced or transmitted in any form or by any means, electronic or mechanical, including photocopying, recording or by any information storage and retrieval system without permission in writing from the Publisher.

Library of Congress
Catalog Card Number: 83-82026

ISBN: 0-8091-2599-4

Published by Paulist Press
545 Island Road, Ramsey, N.J. 07446

Printed and bound in the
United States of America

Contents

To my mother and father

Preface

The conceptual framework of this book is influenced especially by the writings of Alfred North Whitehead, Michael Polanyi and their followers. My purpose, however, is not primarily to give an exposition of their thought, but rather to address central issues in science and religion. I have at times employed the ideas and terminology of these and other scholars to whom I am indebted in a flexible and syncretistic fashion. Consequently, I wish to express at the outset my deep gratitude to them for providing the tools I needed to focus on the problem of science and religion in a manner that may not always be in complete harmony with their own approaches.

I would also like to thank Jude Daly for typing the manuscript, Diane Yeager for critically reading a major portion of it, and Anthony Tambasco for proofreading. Finally, thanks are due especially to the many students who have helped me through their questions and criticisms to shape the ideas presented here.

Introduction

Does the universe have any purpose? Is the emergence of life anything more than a cosmic accident? Was there any intelligence operative in the universe prior to the appearance of man? Is life anything more than atoms and molecules? Is mind anything else than the result of complex movements of the physical and chemical components of the brain? Is there any divine influence present in nature? Is evolution moving in any meaningful direction? Do our individual lives have any ultimate significance in the unfathomable depths of cosmic time and space?

These are a few of the questions that modern science has raised for those of us who believe or hope that there is indeed some final meaning to our lives in the universe. These are not new questions. They have been with us for some time, and they have inspired a number of responses. But many of these responses have been reactionary repudiations of science itself. Others have been intellectually shallow. And still others have been intellectually inaccessible to sincere and able inquirers.

The present work is intended for any intelligent reader who by some acquaintance with the exciting discoveries of modern science may have asked some of the questions raised above. I shall attempt to make presentable to such a questioner the view that our universe is not without purpose and that there is absolutely nothing in the scientific approach that contradicts the essence of a religious interpretation of reality. Instead there is much in scientific discovery and speculation that may help us to understand religion in a new and adventurous way.

For a number of years now I have been teaching a course on science and religion to undergraduates. In doing so I have always had the objective of preparing my students to read in a critical fashion contemporary scientific literature much of which rejects religion as superstition. As I have provided instruction in the complexities of Alfred North Whitehead's and Michael Polanyi's urbane critiques of scientific materialism, I have wished fervently that larger numbers of people could be exposed to their sanity. This book is an attempt to present some of their ideas to a larger audience. Almost without exception I have found that students who have taken the effort to become acquainted with these impressive philosophers have felt deeply rewarded. My hope is that readers of this book may be tantalized to probe further themselves.

It is, of course, difficult to discuss the ways of thinking about the universe that one finds in Whitehead and Polanyi (and their philosophical followers) without being somewhat "academic" in one's presentation. Much is lost when we try to dilute their thought for the purpose of easy clarity. So while the present work is introductory in nature, I shall try to maintain a scholarly level of discussion without being overly pedantic.

This book is my own personal synthesis, heavily informed by Whitehead and Polanyi (and numerous others as well), but not slavishly repetitive of their ideas. It is both a constructive and a critical attempt to engage the central issues in science and religion today.

Let me confess at the very outset that I think it is possible to reconcile the human hope for some cosmic purpose with what modern science has told us about nature. In a broad sense at least, religion is not opposed to science. The essence of "religion" is a basic confidence that the "ultimate environment" of our lives is trustworthy and fulfilling rather than indifferent or hostile toward us. What I mean more specifically by this "ultimate environment" as an encompassing, transcendent sphere of redemptive care will have to await discussion at a later point. However, I think it is important that I state clearly at the outset the direction in which I am moving. I am going to argue that there is nothing in evolutionary theory, molecular biology or recent physics, or any of the natural sciences for that matter, that rules out a religious interpretation of the universe in the sense that I have just described "religion." Furthermore, I think that the sciences are completely congruous with religious symbolism and that we can restate the religious vision in a fresh manner by a study of the universe of modern science. In supporting these statements I do not think I will have to manipulate any of the commonly accepted ideas presented by the sciences. I am deeply respectful toward, indeed in awe of, what science has produced especially in the decades since Darwin's *Origin of Species* was published (1859). And I have no intention of trying to force scientific discoveries to conform to the religious hypothesis.

Perhaps I can do no more than point out the *congruity* of the religious view with the findings of science. I cannot, nor can anyone else, give a scientific demonstration of the validity of the religious hypothesis. Much discussion in science and religion has been sidetracked by the supposition that one can place religious in the same context as scientific ways of knowing. It must be acknowledged that religious assertions are not verifiable or falsifiable, at least in the same manner as scientific propositions are. The religious conviction that the universe is at heart, in its transcendent depths, a graceful, caring, enlivening environment is in a different order of discourse from scientific hypotheses concerning, for example, how species evolved or how matter is converted into energy. So, regardless of how one would assess the truth-status of religious ideas, they do not fall neatly within the realm of propositions that we associate with science.

In the past, of course, numerous scientific thinkers have expressed skepticism about religion because its assertions are not verifiable or falsifiable in the same experimental sense as are scientific assertions. And such suspicion is understandable because religious people have tried often to place their own convictions on the same level as scientific views about the universe, as competing hypotheses. This is essentially what the so-called "creationists" do. Taking the biblical story of creation literally, as though it were in the same family of propositions as scientific statements, creationism sees modern scientifically based views of the cosmos as exclusive of and antagonistic toward biblical religion. The creationist position not only vilifies the legitimate work of dedicated scientists; what is more, it suppresses the essential insight of religion that we may trust the universe, including the human mind and its capacity to grasp rationally the nature of things.

As I shall take it in this book, the central core of religious consciousness is a fundamental trust, primordially expressed in symbols and stories, that reality is ultimately caring. The intuition of divine care is intrinsic to, but not exclusive to, biblical religion. In their essence most if not all religious faiths express a confidence that in spite of the overwhelming presence of chaos, tragedy, suffering, and death, this universe is grounded in an ultimate environment in which the negative is conquered by the power of the positive. The manner in which religious consciousness expresses its intimation of such an ultimate context of meaning is primarily through symbolic and mythic modes of thought and language which differ from culture to culture. The creation story in the Book of Genesis in the Bible, for example, is a culturally specific symbolic and mythic rather than scientific expression of basic trust. One meaning of the story is that our immediate world is a gift freely given by ultimate reality (Yahweh), and that our response to this gift should be one of gratitude and stewardship. This is not the only meaning that scholars have seen in the creation story. (There, are, for example, covenantal and soteriological motifs as well.) But it will serve to illustrate my point that the symbolic and mythic language of religion cannot be appreciated if it is placed in the same class of propositions as those we might find in a biology textbook. The purpose of the creation story is not to give us scientific information about the details of the world's origin. Instead its objective is to awaken the religious participant to the possibility that beyond his or her immediate environment there is an ultimate one which is decisively giving and caring. Its intention is to stimulate consciousness toward the view that being is not one-dimensional, that it is not totally exhausted in its immediate physical manifestations. It proclaims that there is another dimension deeper than and more encompassing than what is immediately available to our comprehension. And it proposes that this other dimension is a gracious source of meaning and purpose for our lives in the immediate environment of nature and history.

However, we are forced to ask earnestly today: Is this intuition of cosmic care consistent with the findings of modern science? And if so, how? If our universe is influenced by any cosmic purpose, how would we know it and what shape would it take in nature and history? These are the questions we must address.

If indeed there is a transcendent ground of cosmic purpose we must humbly admit that we could not get our minds around it in any secure or final fashion. It would "comprehend" us, but we would not be able to comprehend it. And yet, in some mode of consciousness or other, our minds would have to make contact with this encompassing purpose, or it with us, if we are to talk about it at all. What would this mode of consciousness be, and what would be its relation to scientific knowledge?

In spite of the spurious connotations the term will probably have for many readers, I shall use the word "faith" to refer to this non-comprehending intuition of ultimate meaning. I shall attempt to show that the word "faith" may be understood as the mode of consciousness whereby we open ourselves to being grasped by a more comprehensive dimension of reality than the mind itself can objectively master. It is a mode of consciousness which will inevitably arouse the suspicion of those who adhere to what has been called "the epistemology of control" according to which nothing may be called real unless it can be grasped objectively by the methods of science.[1] "Faith" requires the renunciation of the epistemology of control. And such asceticism is not very appealing within the contemporary academic setting. Therefore, I shall not be surprised if my reference to faith should evoke feelings of uneasiness in some readers even at this very early phase of our inquiry.

Still I cannot divorce my discussion of the cosmos from

considerations of the possible role of faith in opening up levels of reality otherwise inaccessible. Especially if our universe is evolutionary and hierarchical, as I shall argue, the role of faith in making us aware of further possible emergent dimensions cannot be disregarded. Through "faith" our human consciousness acknowledges its limitedness and at the same time allows itself to be taken up into a higher or deeper dimension of reality wherein it is given its ultimate purpose in the scheme of things. Accordingly, if purpose is indeed a reality in our universe, it lies beyond the control of both our ordinary and our scientific modes of cognition. This would explain its elusiveness, its inaccessibility, its unobtrusiveness. There is, therefore, a certain wager or risk involved in our entrusting ourselves to a teleological (= purposeful) vision of things. For we may never hope to lay out the nature of this vision with the same degree of clarity and certitude with which we set forth our scientific judgments about nature. We simply cannot "master" any supposed teleological dimension in the cosmos, and so we may be tempted to turn away altogether from consideration of its possibility. I think science is correct in its *methodical* exclusion of teleological hypotheses from its own rendition of the universe. For if a teleological dimension does exist it would lie beyond the objectifying, controlling technique of scientific knowing. The vital question, though, is whether scientific knowing is the only legitimate mode of knowing. Or is there room for faith? I shall propose throughout this book that a hierarchical view of the universe will allow us to clarify how faith and scientific knowledge can coexist and complement each other in our universe. But I make no pretense of exposing clearly and distinctly what nature's purpose may be. In the final analysis, as Whitehead teaches us, clarity and distinctness do not necessarily give us reality in its fundamental and concrete aspects. Perhaps we need symbols and myths to put us in touch with reality in its deeper dimensions. This is the wager I shall propose that we take.

1.

The Problem of Nature and Purpose

The central issue in science and religion today is whether nature in its evolution has any purpose or ultimate meaning. All the other questions that cluster around the topic of science and religion converge on that of nature and purpose. Questions such as whether the language of "faith" has any authority in a scientific age, or whether mind and life are reducible to atoms and molecules, whether only the tangible is real, whether the human person is anything more than a complex physico-chemical mechanism, whether we are free or determined, whether there is any "objective" truth to the symbols and myths of religion—all of these questions are asked at all only because what is fundamentally at issue is whether there is an ultimate context that gives meaning to cosmic process and significance to our lives in this process. The interest that such questions arouse in us is generated primarily by the impingement they have on our own wondering whether there is any basis in reality for our sense of significance. It is questionable whether our own lives can be seriously taken as deeply meaningful unless the cosmic context of these lives is itself imbued with purpose. Thus the problem of nature and purpose is not merely an academic one; it flows from our deepest and most personal concerns as to whether we really belong to the universe, or rather must awaken to our utter solitude, our "fundamental isolation."[1]

Several decades ago, the American philosopher, W.T. Stace, wrote that religion

> . . . can get on with any sort of astronomy, geology, biology, physics. But it cannot get on with a purposeless and senseless world. If the scheme of things is purposeless and meaningless, then the life of man is purposeless and meaningless too. Everything is futile, all effort is in the end worthless.[2]

For some time, however, influential scientific thinkers have insisted that the findings of astronomy, geology, biology and physics rule out the hypothesis of cosmic purpose, or at least render it very dubious. If they are correct, then religion, no matter how lyrical or comforting, has no basis in reality and should be abandoned by all honest, truth-loving persons. Science seems to have made questionable any religious affirmation of ultimate meaning.

I agree with Stace that the central issue is that of cosmic purpose. Unless there is some purpose to the "scheme of things" it seems doubtful whether the individual can consistently and coherently attribute meaning to his or her own existence either. The universe must somehow support us if our own will to meaning is to find any satisfaction. I find it difficult to understand those philosophers who hold that the individual's life can have meaning even if the universe as a whole is void of purpose. If our environing context is indifferent or hostile to us, I do not see how we have a chance of salvaging any ultimately satisfying meaning for ourselves. We are so intricately connected with our universe that any "simple location" of our own existence, any setting it apart from the totality in which we are embedded, will surely skew our self-understanding. And if the universe to which science says we are organically tied is pervasively purposeless, how can our individual lives avoid being infected by the insignificance that runs through the whole?

And yet there are some philosophers who hold that our chances for personal meaning are not jeopardized, but are even enhanced, by our living in a purposeless universe. E.D. Klemke, just to give one recent but representative example, clearly illustrates this point of view. He begins by observing that there is no "evidence" for any purpose in the universe:

> From the standpoint of present evidence, evaluational components such as meaning or purpose are not to be found in the universe as objective aspects of it. Such values are the result of human evaluation. With respect to them, we must say that the universe is valueless; it is *we* who evaluate, upon the basis of our subjective preferences. Hence, we do not discover values such as meaning to be inherent within the universe. Rather, we "impose" such values upon the universe.[3]

And in a spirit of honesty Klemke gives us the epistemology (that is, the view of what constitutes true knowledge) which undergirds his skepticism about meaning in the universe:

> ... I here maintain what I hold throughout the rest of my existence, both philosophically and simply as a living person. I can accept only what is comprehensible to me; i.e., that which is within the province of actual or possible experience, or that for which I find some sound reasons or evidence. Upon these grounds, I must reject any notion of meaning which is bound with the necessity of faith in some mysterious, utterly unknowable entity. If my life should turn out to be less happy thereby, then I shall have to endure it as such. As Shaw once said: "The fact that a believer is happier than a skeptic is no more to the point than the fact that a drunken man is happier than a sober one. The happiness of credulity is a cheap and dangerous quality."[4]

I admire this statement for its clarity and the intellectual honesty that underlies it. If indeed it is true that there is no ultimate purpose to things, then we should face up to this fact, no matter how much it hurts. (Here I shall not pursue the question as to *why* we should do so.) But then Klemke goes on, with his usual pointedness, to express the view which I would like the reader to ponder:

> An objective meaning—that is, one which is inherent within the universe or dependent upon external agencies—would, frankly, leave me cold. It would not be *mine*. It would be an outer, neutral thing, rather than an inner, dynamic achievement. I, for one, am *glad* that the universe has no meaning, for thereby is *man all the more glorious.* I willingly accept the fact that external meaning is non-existent (or if existent, certainly not apparent), for this leaves me free to *forge my own meaning.*[5]

Klemke, I think, is an adequate representative of those who argue for the meaningfulness of the individual's life even though the universe may be empty of meaning itself. Therefore any attempt to construct a vision of the universe (a cosmology) in which there is some over-arching meaning (teleology) must address itself to the kinds of claims Klemke is making. I shall briefly isolate three of these claims in the remainder of this chapter, and draw out their deeper implications in subsequent sections of the book.

1. First there is an epistemological assumption that we should give our assent to no proposition unless there is adequate experiential (empirical and scientific) evidence for it or unless it is capable of being "comprehended." Of course the proposition that the universe is meaningful is indeed unreceptive to experimental verification and falsification. Therefore, Klemke discards teleology as unacceptable. Later on I shall present a hierarchical model of the universe according to which we must re-evaluate the whole notion of "comprehension."[6] In this hierarchical view we shall acknowledge that a higher level may comprehend a lower, but a lower cannot comprehend a higher. If purpose is intrinsic to a hierarchical universe, then it would be located at a higher level than that of human consciousness. Thus it would by nature be beyond our conscious comprehension. The obvious question, then, is whether

Klemke's epistemological assumption that all of reality must be accessible to our human faculties of comprehension is necessarily appropriate to the nature of the universe. Should there in fact exist a teleological dimension to the cosmos, comprehension (in the sense of getting our minds around something) could not occur. Instead what I earlier called "faith" would be the appropriate stance of consciousness with respect to ultimate meaning. Faith is an attitude of acknowledging the limits of comprehension and of opening ourselves to being comprehended by that which transcends us. To make our own intellectual possessiveness the criterion of all that is real is an example of the "epistemology of control." And as Huston Smith has stated: "An epistemology that aims relentlessly at control rules out the possibility of transcendence in principle."[7]

Klemke holds that ultimate meaning is beyond comprehension (beyond verification or falsification). Thus far I would not care to argue, though what precisely is meant by "ultimate meaning" or by "verification" could be more carefully pondered. What I am most concerned with is the inference Klemke draws from his observations on the elusiveness of any hypothetical ultimate meaning: if it cannot be comprehended, then its reality is in question. Behind this proposition there lies the assumption that the human mind is the highest level in the cosmic hierarchy. By a "hierarchical cosmos" I mean a universe in which there are a multiplicity of systems, levels, dimensions or fields so arranged that the higher or greater exercise an integrating and organizing influence over the components that constitute the subordinate levels. For example, the living cell organizes and integrates the subsidiary molecules in what is an obviously "hierarchical" fashion. And as we shall see later, the human mind exercises a hierarchically integrating influence over the biological, neurological, and chemical processes in the brain and body. Klemke, like many modern philosophers, assumes that there are no higher organizing and integrating fields of influence more comprehensive than the human mind. And it is to this point of view that much of the speculation and reflection in the present book will be addressed. How do we know that our own minds are not superseded by, transcended by and comprehended by a still higher level (or by higher levels)? How do we know that we do not live in a hierarchical universe in which our consciousness is not the supreme organizational field?

It makes all the difference in the world, as we speculate on the issue of nature and purpose, where we locate our human consciousness in terms of the hierarchical universe. Is it the highest level or is it perhaps relatively low on a cosmic scale of gradations of comprehending dimensions? Because of its bearing on the question of purpose, therefore, much of this book will focus on the feasibility and legitimacy of hierarchical thinking. Consequently, I shall repeatedly make reference to what I shall call the "hierarchical principle" as the axiom to guide our reflections. This principle is formulated as follows: a higher level can comprehend a lower, but the lower cannot comprehend the higher.[8] We shall flesh this principle out as we move forward.

2. A second striking aspect of Klemke's position is his assertion that the universe is inherently *valueless*. Klemke is consistent when he claims, therefore, that the universe is purposeless. For what renders a process purposeful is its orientation toward value. And where there are no value-oriented occurrences there can be no ultimate meaning. What is interesting about the claim that the universe is intrinsically valueless is that this view is usually rooted in speculation influenced by modern science. It is true that ancient Greek atomists excluded any final cause (any ultimate goal or good) in their explanation of the cosmos, and ancient tragedy also questioned whether the universe is purposeful. But with the exception of a few skeptics, prior to the seventeenth century most philosophy as well as religion treated the universe as inherently value-laden. What rendered it valuable was the commonly accepted view that it was permeated by Mind, Intelligence, Reason, Logos, Torah, God, Spirit, Presence. The cosmos, as Jacob Needleman puts it, was perceived as a *teaching*. And the proper response to this instructive cosmos, itself seen as the embodiment of Wisdom, was a reverential obedience. The individual's mind was seen as

a microcosmic version of the Cosmic Mind, and so the authentic life for the individual required his or her attunement to the intelligence of the cosmic totality. The idea that the universe is intrinsically valueless was the last thought that could have occurred to traditional minds.[9]

Whatever happened that makes it possible now for philosophers like Klemke to state with such ingenuousness that the cosmos is intrinsically devoid of value, and therefore of purpose? Clearly it is the expulsion of mind from the cosmic totality and its relegation to our individual craniums.[10] It has been pointed out that prior to the Enlightenment, the human mind was seen as a mirror of the cosmos. That is, its function was to reflect the intelligibility and value that are intrinsic to the universe. After the Enlightenment, however, it is perhaps best envisaged as a lamp. The human mind is the source of, rather than a reflection of, whatever meaning exists. If mind exists at all today (and some question whether it has any intrinsic reality because of its intangibility) it resides locally and tenuously only in our brains. According to some modern scientific thinkers there was no mind in the cosmos at all prior to the emergence of man in evolution. G.G. Simpson, the famous biologist of evolution, for example, starkly implies this conclusion:

> Man is the result of a purposeless and natural process that did not have him in mind. He was not planned.
> . . .
> Man plans and has purposes. Plan, purpose, goal, all absent in evolution to this point, enter with the coming of man and are inherent in the new evolution which is confined to him.
> . . .
> Discovery that the universe apart from man or before his coming lacks and lacked any purpose or plan has the inevitable corollary that the workings of the universe cannot provide any automatic, universal, eternal, or absolute ethical criteria of right and wrong.[11]

If the universe is itself mindless, then it cannot provide a basis for our valuations. Our own minds are left isolated, stranded in a strange and hostile environment which offers no support in our own quest for meaning. Our minds, unaided and alone, have to illuminate the cosmos which itself is void of light.

What happened that brought about this sense that mind and cosmos are alien to one another? Was it simply the rise of science in the last three centuries? Certainly science has given us pictures of vast tracts of lifeless and unconscious space. Physics, astronomy, chemistry and geology as well as biology have considerably altered our cosmographies. Science has methodically excluded consideration of value and purpose from the field of its inquiry. Moreover, it deals with the quantitative more than the qualitative aspects of things. It abstracts altogether from those questions which interest us "existentially," such as what, if any, is the meaning of our lives. For these reasons we may legitimately suspect that science has been a major factor in the turn away from teleology. W.T. Stace, whom I quoted earlier, even goes so far as to put the whole burden of modernity's turn away from belief in cosmic purpose on the seventeenth century's preoccupation with "how" questions to the exclusion of "why" questions:

> The real turning point between the medieval age of faith and the modern age of unfaith came when the scientists of the seventeenth century turned their backs upon what used to be called "final causes." The final cause of a thing or event meant the purpose which it was supposed to serve in the universe, its cosmic purpose. What lay back of this was the presupposition that there is a cosmic order or plan, and that everything that exists could in the last analysis be explained in terms of its place in this cosmic plan, that is, in terms of its purpose.[12]

Though Galileo, Kepler and Newton did not personally deny the reality of purpose, Stace insists that they made this notion useless in terms of what science aims at, "namely prediction and control." Science turned exclusively to the search for material and mechanical causes and turned its back on final causes. Hence increasingly modern thought, affected by the methods of scientific inquiry, has issued us a picture of the universe in which purpose plays no part. Stace continues:

> You can draw a sharp line across the history of Europe dividing it into two epochs of very unequal length. The line passes through the life time of Galileo. European man before Galileo—whether ancient pagan or more recent Christian— thought of the world as controlled by plan and purpose. After Galileo European man thinks of it as utterly purposeless.[13]

Even allowing for some rhetorical exaggeration by Stace, I think we must dig much deeper than he has to find the fundamental causes of the picture of a universe void of value, mind and purpose. Prior to the emergence of modern science, the roots of its disengagement of nature from mind and value were already present in our Western cultural heritage. These roots go deep down into ancient mythologies that have for centuries nurtured our philosophies and spiritualities. It is not surprising that what we call "modern science" should also have failed to escape their nourishing influence. I am referring especially to the myth of dualism. And I think some understanding of dualistic mythology, philosophy and psychology may help explain the caesura of which Stace is speaking and the divorce of mind from nature that gives Klemke's ideas their essential structure.

Dualism is the mythic, religious or philosophical view that separates spirit from matter and mind from body. A mythical version of dualistic thinking may be found in what Paul Ricoeur calls the "myth of the exiled soul."[14] This myth, like most important myths, is a theodicy. It is an attempt to explain where evil comes from and how we may escape from it. It came to expression in ancient Orphism, Manichaeism, Gnosticism, and Zoroastrianism and has persisted down through the centuries in religious and philosophical forms of expression. It tells of how the soul, having its origin in the world of the spirit, strays here below into the (evil) realm of matter. The soul takes up a temporary dwelling in a "body" which functions as a prison and as the source of evil desires and suffering. Recognizing its distinct status, the soul ideally resists being absorbed into the bodily casing derived from inferior matter. Through various forms of asceticism, renunciation of instinct, contemplation of the spiritual and the ideal, and eventually through death, the soul migrates back to its original home.

This is a powerful and touching myth, not least because it gives a rather tidy answer to the perennial human problem of suffering and evil. It is also appealing because it preserves the sense of our special significance over against the material world. It is not remarkable, therefore, that this myth has been so durable throughout our history, including the history of ideas. In antiquity, Plato, and, at the beginning of the modern age, Descartes, stand out as the best known figures in the history of philosophical dualism. Numerous thinkers have been shaped by this Platonic-Cartesian tradition. Recently, for example, one of its most outspoken contemporary apologists, Hywel D. Lewis, has recapitulated the arguments on behalf of dualism. Lewis states that there is a radical difference between mental states and physical states and that the essence of dualism consists in this distinction.[15] Dualism explains why we spontaneously value sentient and conscious beings more than inanimate objects, namely, because there is an added higher component in the former that does not exist in the latter:

> . . . we seem compelled to recognize some reality which cannot be itself described in strictly physical terms, however close the involvement may be with material conditions. It is for these reasons that we speak of cruelty to animals but not to pieces of wood or stone. . . . This is the obvious divide from which dualism takes its course.[16]

Furthermore, dualism gives legitimacy to what we call "inner" experience.[17] It provides a basis for the sense of freedom and dignity without which a genuine humanism would collapse. So numerous are its advantages that Lewis wonders why anyone would challenge dualism. Gilbert Ryles' famous critique of dualism, for example, is unsatisfactory since in the final analysis it differs little from the old-fashioned materialism of behaviorists like J.B. Watson, for whom distinct "inner" states of awareness do not exist.[18] In general, it is "irritating" to Lewis that so many distinguished philosophers fail to recognize the appropriateness of "the Platonic-Cartesian way."[19] Our own experience of our sentience and consciousness should be enough to vindicate the dualistic position.

Yet I must emphasize that while dualism seeks to preserve the core of our humanness from being lost in matter, ironically it prepares the way for the materialist interpretation of the world it seeks to avoid in the first place. For by placing the soul or mind in a sphere radically different from that of physical reality, dualism abandons the physical universe to the realm of the spiritless and mindless. And it is fundamentally the mindlessness of nature that renders it incapable of sustaining purpose.

Of course one may imagine, as did the natural theologians of the eighteenth and nineteenth centuries, that a divine mechanic situated outside of the mindless world-machine could manipulatively direct it in a "purposive" way. But this view itself collapsed eventually because it was not a truly teleological one. If the world of nature is radically purposeful it is not sufficient that its purpose be extrinsic to it. Instead any teleological influence must be felt intimately by all aspects of the world. This means that the fundamental constituents of nature must have built into them a quality of receptivity to transcendent meaning that would allow them to be brought into the sphere of influence of any supposed universal teleological principle. The name I shall give to this hypothesized quality of receptivity to meaning is "mentality." And in the following two chapters I shall ask whether it is scientifically and philosophically legitimate to attribute "mentality" to every aspect of the universe. My position will be that unless the universe is pervasively "mental" there would be no possibility of any global meaning taking up residence within it. For this reason a critique of the dualism which separates mentality from the physical universe by exiling it to the sphere of human consciousness must be the first step in any effort to present a teleological picture of the universe.

The consequences of the dualistic siphoning of mind from nature are not terribly dramatic until the age of science. For in archaic and ancient settings reality seemed to be almost completely permeated with a spirit of vitality. Rivers, plants, the earth, humanity, the climate—the entire environment—gave the impression of being saturated with life. Panvitalism, according to Hans Jonas, was the common view.[20] Where there was an apparent absence of vitality, as in a corpse, there was a tendency to deny the reality of any dead matter and to look upon death itself as an illusion. But once science uncovered the pervasive lifelessness of the physical universe, and pointed out how precariously infinitesimal is the quantity of life and mind, then more dramatic consequences began to flow from our dualistic heritage. Mind and life are now experienced as strangers, as anomalies, as accidents that have erupted on a landscape of deadness and mindlessness that is unsympathetic with or at the most neutral toward them. Having segregated mind from matter, spirit from the body, and life from the inert, dualism bequeaths to us a new problematic that has given contemporary science its characteristic methodological ideal. Instead of being confronted with the ancient problem of how to explain death if everything around us exudes life, we now have to apologize for the precarious fact of life (and consciousness) if everything around us in our universe is intrinsically dead and mindless. Jonas elaborates on this ironic twist of problematics:

> Death is the natural thing, life the problem. From the physical sciences there spread over the conception of all existence an ontology whose model entity is pure matter, stripped of all features of life. What at the animistic stage was not even discovered has in the meantime conquered the vision of reality, entirely ousting its counterpart. The tremendously enlarged universe of modern cosmology is conceived as a field of inanimate masses and forces which operate according to the laws of inertia and of quantitative distribution in space. This denuded substratum of all reality could only be arrived at through a progressive expurgation of vital features from the physical record and through strict abstention from projecting into its image our own felt aliveness.

This means that the lifeless has become the knowable par excellence and is for that reason also considered the true and only foundation of reality. It is the "natural" as well as the original state of things. Not only in terms of relative quantity but also in terms of ontological genuineness, nonlife is the rule, life the puzzling exception in physical existence.[21]

As a result of this inverted theoretical situation, Jonas concludes, ". . . it is the existence of life within a mechanical universe which now calls for an explanation, and explanation has to be in terms of the lifeless."[22]

The explanation of the "living" in terms of non-living stuff has become the ideal of much modern scientific inquiry. It is obvious to many, for example, that biology is reducible to physics and chemistry, and, therefore, that life is reducible to inanimate matter. The amazing advances in molecular biology blur the traditional hierarchical distinctions between man, animal, plant and mineral; and the neurophysiological "explanation" of human consciousness in terms of the components and machinations of the brain even more dramatically illustrates how pure "matter" has assumed dominance in any attempt to make sense of our universe and its manifestations.

It is the dualism of soul and body, spirit and nature, mind and matter that has made possible the shift of problematics from that of how to explain death if everything is alive, to that of how to explain life if everything is dead. Dualism is the pivotal mythic and philosophical construct on which this inversion has turned. While dualism may have been an important factor in our coming to vivid awareness of the faculty of mentality which makes us aware of our special status in the world, it has simultaneously purged nature outside of ourselves of the qualities of mind and aliveness that we experience in the subtlety of our own conscious activity. It has therefore exorcised the cosmos of the mentality without which it would remain impervious to any deep incarnation of transcendent meaning. It has given rise to what Paul Tillich has called an "ontology of death."[23] Anything that is not part of our subjective experience is relegated to a world "out there" and is denuded of the vitality associated with thought and experience. This world outside of our own minds is then envisaged as inhabited only by dead, inert and passive material objects.

The bifurcation of reality into two such disparate regions culminated in Descartes' noted distinction of *res cogitans* (mind) and *res extensa* (matter). The influence of the dualistic myth and metaphysics on the birth and growth of modern science has been amply documented,[24] and I cannot trace the whole story here. It is enough only to point out that the inertness bequeathed to matter by dualism has become the basis upon which the quantification of physical reality and motion in Newtonian and Cartesian physics has been constructed. And perhaps we may even say that without the dualistic premise modern science as we know it could not have developed as rapidly as it has.

It is also true, though, that dualism still lurks behind the dominant contemporary philosophies of nature in which matter remains essentially mindless and lifeless. It is dualism that, in the final analysis, provides the background for the present day attempts to specify or explain biotic and conscious operations in terms of the sciences (physics and chemistry) that deal with the allegedly inanimate. Without the sphere of unconscious and lifeless chunks of matter delineated by dualism such a methodological ideal (which animates current efforts especially in biology to find the physico-chemical "secret" of life) could hardly have taken hold in modern scientific thought. In a curious way we owe a great deal to what is perhaps a serious mistake in cosmology.[25]

Standing at the end of the history of this dualism it is easy for us to see why any attribution of "mentality" (and therefore of purposefulness) to nature will be dismissed as romantic anthropomorphism by philosophers like Klemke. By expelling anything that resembles feeling, experience or perceptivity from the fundamental "building-blocks" of nature, modern thought has also eliminated the possibility of attributing purpose to the universe. It has rightly recognized that without a vein of "mentality" in the universe there can be no purpose either. And so, by rejecting the alliance of nature and mind, it has removed to that extent the feasibility of our searching for purpose in the world of nature. For where there is no dimension of "mind" there can be no implantation of aim or purpose either.

In turn, the rejection of a teleological universe has led in many cases to doubt about any human purpose whatsoever. Needless to say, there has been a close connection all along between the modern experience of meaninglessness and the development of the picture of an impersonal universe that gives no backing to our projects. The same dualistic myths that have made us feel exceptional have also led to our sense of alienation from nature and purpose.

It is possible in theory to anticipate, therefore, the enormous implications that a new alliance of nature and mind might have for the contemporary crisis of meaning. Nothing less imposing than the significance of our lives is bound up with the quest for a union of mind and nature established on solid grounds compatible with reason, common sense and science. If we could grasp somehow that our subjectivity is a blossoming forth of nature itself, and not some enigmatic "nothingness" or separate substance over against nature, we would have at least the context in which to discuss once again the question of nature and purpose.[26]

The basis for a synthetic vision of mind and nature is worked out most comprehensively by Alfred North Whitehead, and we shall investigate his ideas in an introductory fashion in Chapter 3.

3. There is yet a third element in Klemke's proposal. It is his optimism that we can tolerate and accommodate ourselves to a purposeless universe. It is his bold post-Enlightenment assertion that each of us as individuals is capable of suffusing our lives with whatever meaning we need. In fact, Klemke holds, the more naked the universe is of purpose the less interference we would have from it in forging our own meanings. Whatever meaning traditional myth, philosophy and religion saw in the cosmos, we now recognize as the creations or projections of the people that inhabited it. We should now, in

the spirit of modernity, fully acknowledge and accept our own creative role in such projections. We should give credit where credit is due—to ourselves. The individual is radically responsible for his or her own life's meaning since the universe has no help to offer on this score.

Again, the way toward this kind of thinking was paved by dualism. It is the irrepressible presence of dualism that allows us to think that our mental activity is not really a part of or continuous with nature. Dualistic mythology is the cultural backdrop for Klemke's Cartesian-Sartrean sense of his mind's being in a separate ontological category from mindless nature. And like Sartre, Camus, Russell and other cosmic pessimists before him, Klemke seems unaware of the tenacious hold that the dualistic way of organizing the world may have over his consciousness. In the pages that follow I shall give considerable attention to the way in which the dualistic separation of value from the universe has structured the whole question of science and religion. And that is why I shall repeatedly question whether we are required to adapt ourselves to the dualistic mythology that has been such a powerful influence in the history of culture and thought.

Conclusion

In order to entertain the hypothesis that there is cosmic purpose one must assume that nature and mind are somehow interwoven. If the universe of nature were completely void of what we shall call "mentality," it would not be capable of receiving or sustaining any intelligible orientation toward value, that is, any purpose. Once physical reality has been pictured as impermeable to mind, the stage is already set for estranging the individual from the universe, for divorcing purpose from nature. On such a stage there appears the modern philosophy of scientific materialism.

2.

Scientific Materialism

Scientists tell us that our universe came to be in an explosion of unimaginable proportions fifteen to twenty billion years ago. Since this "Big Bang" galaxies, stars and planets have gradually congealed out of the gases released by that unique and momentous cosmic event. A continual expansion outward into space of these heavenly bodies has covered distances measurable only in light years unfathomable by our feeble imaginations. About five billion years ago our planet Earth spun out into orbit around the sun, an insignificant star in one of billions of galaxies each containing possibly billions of other suns and their satellites. Since its birth the Earth's surface has gradually cooled and has become covered with large bodies of water and land. Two or three billion years ago primitive forms of life appeared that eventually evolved into plants, protozoa, reptiles, birds, mammals and finally humans.

A.I. Oparin gives us a way to picture the expanses of time required for the eventual evolution of life and man. Imagine the chronicle of evolution on our (roughly five billion years old) planet as represented in ten large volumes of five hundred pages each. Each page would stand for a million years. Any discussion of the fossilized remains of animals and plants would not take place until the very last volume. We may conjecture that very primitive forms of life began to appear in the seventh or eighth volume. But we have no fossil record of these hypothetical forebears of our biosphere. The first half of the tenth volume would deal with the development of plants and amphibious animals. But it would not be until sixty or seventy pages from the end of this final five hundred page book that we would read about reptiles reaching the height of their development. Around page 465 birds and beasts become the dominant characters in our story. *And the history of human beings has to be told in the last page or two of the final volume!*[1]

Is this evolutionary process a purposeful one? Is this a teleological universe? Is it seeking out some end? Is it in the process of realizing some value or aim? May it be portrayed as the unfolding of a meaningful story in which we each play a significant part? Or are such narrative portrayals without any foundation in reality itself? Are they sheer projections as Klemke and many others suspect?

I shall argue in this book that such a "narrative" interpretation of nature, one that discerns a sort of story-line in nature, can only be called a projection if nature itself is dualistically segregated from those events that we call mental. I shall agree with Whitehead that we must understand mental occurrences as an intrinsic aspect of nature. And once we do so we need no longer envisage our own myths, hopes and intuitions of ultimate meaning as extra-natural occurrences. Rather they may be seen as the straining of the cosmos itself, at this "hominized" phase in its evolution, for a further unraveling of the evolutionary chronicle.

It is not clear to everyone, however, that our own mentality is itself a blossoming forth of nature itself. As we saw in the previous chapter the spirit of dualistic mythology continues to pressure us into the assumption that acts of consciousness or subjectivity are not part of the continuum of occurrences that constitute the world of nature. And as a result of this vestigial dualism, nature, the world studied by the sciences, is denuded of anything mental—and therefore of the possibility of sustaining any universal meaning. Meaning, which requires expression through the narrative mode of consciousness, appears to dualistic thinking as the concoction of our alienated subjectivity. And our subjectivity, in turn, is then burdened with the task of having to be the radical creator of all stories, rather than being, at least in part, the recipient, vehicle or reader of a universal story. Because stories now appear to be anchorless, flowing as they do from the caprice of a groundless subjectivity, it is little wonder that they provide us with no solid sustenance in our own search for meaning. Unless our stories have a cosmic dimension to them, I doubt whether they can move us deeply or provide the solid ground we need to stand on in order to live with conviction and hope.

Few people would deny that from the very beginnings of consciousness, we humans have been characterized by an ability to conceive purposes and to establish goals for our lives. Furthermore, from very early on, consciousness was itself shaped by myths, one of whose central functions was to spell out a meaningful destiny for people. These myths linked human purpose to an intuited cosmic intelligence. Throughout most of human history, up until three hundred years ago, almost all peoples in all parts of our planet took for granted the intelligibility and purposefulness of the world around them. It was simply assumed that some sort of underlying "presence," "sacred" intelligence, "nous" (mind), "Logos" (reason) (or Brahman, Tao, Torah, Dharma) influences the natural world. We are told by historians and anthropologists that people usually felt "at home" in such a world. A personalized or intelligent cosmos was an apt domicile for the individual minds that mirrored the cosmic intelligence.[2]

However, in the last three hundred years it has become possible for us to think of the universe as bereft of any cosmic mind. Such a stark view would not have been conceivable on such a wide scale until after the seventeenth century. Along with dualistic mythology several developments in scientific thought since the seventeenth century have contributed to the exorcism of mind from nature: first, there is the cosmography of classical (Newtonian) physics picturing our world as composed of inanimate, unconscious bits of "matter" needing only the brute laws of inertia to explain their action; second, the Darwinian theory of evolution with its emphasis on chance, waste and the apparent "impersonality" of natural selection; third, the laws of thermodynamics (and particularly the second law) with the allied cosmological interpretation that our universe is running out of energy available to sustain life, evolution and human consciousness; fourth, the geological and astronomical disclosure of enormous tracts of apparently lifeless space and matter in the universe; fifth, the recent suggestions that life may be reducible to an inanimate chemical basis; and, finally, perhaps most shocking of all, the suspicion that mind may be explained exhaustively in terms of mindless brain chemistry.

Such developments as these have made scientifically-minded people wonder whether it is still possible to speak intelligently of any cosmic intelligence that gives over-arching purpose to the universe. Can we not now explain all the so-called "miracles" of life and mind (and even social behavior) in terms of chemical and genetic composition? When it seems unlikely that life transcends the chains of atoms and molecules that compose it, how can we speak seriously of a "cosmic purpose" or "ultimate meaning" that transcends the universe? Or when it seems unscientific to skim "mind" off of its cerebral underpinnings, why would it be any more likely that we could distinguish a transcendent cosmic intelligence from the physical cosmos itself, or refer to an ultimate environment distinguishable from an immediate one?

Scientific Materialism

We are left, therefore, with three parallel sets of questions:

1. Is life reducible to atoms and molecules?

2. Is mind reducible to brain, which in turn is composed of atoms and molecules?

3. Is the universe as a whole reducible to mindless matter?

Scientific materialism is the philosophy of nature which answers "yes" to all three questions. As defined by one of its contemporary defenders, Harvard's Edward O. Wilson, scientific materialism is ". . . the view that all phenomena in the universe, including the human mind, have a material basis, are subject to the same physical laws, and can be most deeply understood by scientific analysis."[3] Scientific analysis of their "material basis" is the exclusive key to unlocking the mysteries of life, mind and the universe as a whole. This material basis may not necessarily be the crude "brickyard" variety that one finds in eighteenth and nineteenth century science. It may be partially informed by the relativity theory and quantum physics of the twentieth century. Yet it shares with the mechanism of the past the view that any non-material, extraneous causation is ruled out in the constitution of the universe. Obviously any teleological interpretation is thereby excluded in principle. Scientific materialism holds that any true and meaningful knowledge that we may gain about life, mind and the universe can be gotten only through the analytical methods of science. Everything else is sheer speculation if not wishful thinking. Oparin's ten-volume history of the world is a chronicle of the reshuffling of atoms and molecules rather than the story of a world's struggle toward the realization of value or purpose.

Scientific materialists look upon life and mind as "epiphenomena," that is, as secondary and derivative rather than "really real" in themselves. The only real "phenomena" are the "physical" components that make up all things. Even those organisms that act as though they are "alive" or as though they are "thinking" are purely material. Aliveness and thought have no intrinsic reality themselves. They owe their flimsy and precarious "existence" to the combinations of atoms, molecules and cells that make up living and thinking organisms. Living and thinking are simply ways in which pure "matter" acts in certain complex combinations. The fundamental components of living and thinking entities, however, are themselves inanimate and unconscious. Reality, in the fundamental sense, is utterly void of life and mind. And if that is so, then it is also without purpose.

Since the appearance in evolution of life and mind depends upon the proper combinations and interrelations of physical and chemical components, it seems that their "existence" or their "reality" is very thin indeed. We all know by now that if the atomic combinations break down, or if the proper chemical reactions fail to take place, the cell will die or the brain (in which thought seems to dwell) will fail to function, and "mind" will be impaired or it may vanish altogether. It is quite understandable, therefore, that scientific materialists would hold firmly to their doctrine that life and mind are reducible to the entities and processes studied by physics and chemistry. Life and mind are in themselves too elusive, too "epiphenomenal" to be grasped apart from their physiological basis. Therefore, it is tempting to reduce them to this basis, to deny that they have any reality in themselves.

Scientific materialism, almost three centuries old, is still the reigning philosophy of nature. It has been seriously challenged by developments in recent physics, but biology and brain science remain heavily oriented toward a materialist interpretation of life and mind. Popular scientific literature like that of Carl Sagan, Isaac Asimov, Jacob Bronowski, Robert Jastrow, or Stephen Jay Gould is steeped in the premises and preoccupations of scientific materialism. Most popular scientific journals have the same bent. And the major universities of the Western world harbor many influential thinkers who can only be classified as materialists. For many of these thinkers the Democritean summation of reality as nothing more than "atoms and the void" is still an adequate rendition of the fundamental nature of things. For others a more elaborate and contemporary version of the physical world qualifies their naturalistic outlook. But even in the latter case the designation "scientific materialism" seems to be appropriate. So because of the academic credibility that still remarkably adheres to scientific materialism I have chosen to devote much of the present book to a critique of it. Though I think it has been intelligently criticized before, its tenacity in classrooms and bookstores everywhere warrants yet another attempt at exploring its plausibility. I hope not only to add something to the fine critiques that have already been offered, but also to marshal them in a novel and instructive manner.

There are two distinguishable aspects of scientific materialism's challenge to teleology that I would like to address respectively in each of the following two chapters. The first is the assumption by materialism that physical reality is mindless stuff. The second is the analytical obsession with the ideal of explaining phenomena (such as life and mind) solely in terms of their constituent elements. In the following chapter I shall provide a Whiteheadian critique of the view of matter presupposed by scientific materialism. And in Chapter 4 I shall utilize Polanyi's thought in order to expose the logical inadequacy of a reductionist interpretation of life and mind.

3.

Mind in Nature

In *Science and the Modern World,* Alfred North Whitehead wrote of the scientific materialism stemming from the seventeenth century:

> It has held its own as the guiding principle of scientific studies ever since. It is still reigning. Every university in the world organizes itself in accordance with it. No alternative system of organizing the pursuit of scientific truth has been suggested. It is not only reigning, but it is without a rival.
>
> And yet—it is quite unbelievable. This conception of the universe is surely framed in terms of high abstractions, and the paradox only arises because we have mistaken our abstractions for concrete realities.[1]

Scientific materialism, according to Whitehead, is a misrepresentation of the cosmos because it is based on the "fallacy of misplaced concreteness."[2] This fallacy of misplaced concreteness is simply the confusion of abstractions with concrete reality. It is the tendency to take our mental constructs and imaginative models of the world, such as those of the machine, wave or particle, as though they corresponded exactly to the world itself. This is an understandable temptation since we have to simplify things in order even to begin to understand them. But we do not always heed Whitehead's exhortation first to seek simplicity and then to mistrust it.[3] We easily do the first, but tend to balk at the second. I would suggest that we fail to mistrust our over-simplifications for the same reasons that we are inclined toward the epistemology of control. Somehow and for some reason we fear giving up our sense of mastery over the universe. But we do so at great peril to our cosmology and to our general vision of things.

Whitehead's critique of scientific materialism is that it is too abstract. This indictment perhaps sounds strange, since if anything seems concrete it is the collection of allegedly irreducible particles of matter out of which nature is composed according to the materialist's philosophy. What could be more concrete than atoms in the void? The elegant simplicity of the atomist philosophy, or its contemporary equivalents in an updated particle physics or molecular biology, may easily seduce us into the assumption that bits of matter or indivisible mechanisms are the bedrock foundation of reality. And yet, on more careful analysis, they turn out to be "high abstractions."

Why do mindless chunks of matter not qualify for being the ultimate "concrete" constituents of nature? Simply because they are the product of the scientific method's prescinding from certain aspects of the universe with which it is incapable of dealing. These aspects that are left behind (by the use of the machine model and the still dominant particle model) are part of the concrete fabric of the universe, and so any adequate cosmology should advert to them as well. The neglected elements I am referring to are the "qualitative" aspects of things, aspects which escape the net of mechanistic and quantitative modes of understanding. More specifically they are the aspects of beauty, value and importance, none of which fall within the realm of ordinary scientific discussion.

Of course these aspects of the universe that are left out of scientific discussion will be looked upon by the materialist as epiphenomenal, as our own subjective desires projected onto the blank neutrality of the universe. Value seems to fall within the same arena as the so-called "secondary qualities" isolated by classical physics and the philosophy of John Locke. Secondary qualities are those aspects of things which seem to depend for their existence upon the perceiver. Color, taste, smell, sound and touch all require an experiencing subject in which to reside, and so they apparently do not have any "objective" reality to them. They are derived only from the perceiver who cloaks the objects with secondary qualities. Meanwhile the object itself onto which the secondary qualities are projected is said to be made up of "primary qualities." Primary qualities are those features of objects that allegedly exist independently of any experiencing subject. The object's mass, position and momentum, for example, do not seem to depend upon my being present to perceive them. They exist independently of my experience; they endure throughout the process of accidental changes, and, therefore, they seem to be more real, more concrete than the secondary qualities. Scientific materialism usually holds that primary qualities are the concretely real foundation of things and that secondary qualities are the frothy result of our projecting elements of unreliable subjectivity onto them.

The important implication of this distinction of primary from secondary qualities (itself rooted in the mind/matter dualism which we looked at earlier) is that it provides the cosmological basis for a denial that there is any *intrinsic* meaning in the universe independent of meaning-creating individuals. It has become very easy after the seventeenth century to situate the whole notion of meaning or value in the same context as secondary qualities. The values that we cherish and that give our lives whatever meaning they may have seem to depend for their precarious existence upon the sensitivity of evaluators. Our sense of the importance of things, events, persons, and of the universe itself, seems to share with secondary qualities the characteristic of being totally subjective and arbitrary. Accordingly meaning does not appear to be intrinsic to the universe. The cosmos seems inherently vacant of purpose, and teleology is apparently the mere product of our own valuations.

The restriction of value to the realm of subjectivity depends upon a prior separation of our consciousness from the cosmos. This separation has recently been challenged not only by philosophy but also by developments in science itself. Hence our discussion of the issue of purpose in the universe must inquire about the possibility of some other assessment of the relation of mind to nature. It is especially in the thought of Alfred North Whitehead that we may find such an alternative.

Reality as Process

According to Whitehead reality is process. Evolutionary theory has impressed this fact upon us, but it is also one of the most obvious conclusions of modern physics. Ages ago Heraclitus weepingly declared that all is in flux. The Buddha made transiency central to his vision of reality. In this century Henri Bergson taught us how central process is to our inner and outer experience. And even more recently Whitehead has emphasized the dynamic, processive nature both of reality as a whole and also of its constituent elements. According to Whitehead the universe is made up of moments that become and then perish. These moments are linked together in various kinds of series or patterns that build up into all the various objects of our experience. But beneath the apparent stability of these entities there are events, happenings, occasions. In short, there is process.[4]

Today quantum physics has compelled many scientists to conclude that process is the most fundamental fact. Previously we supposed, with materialism, that only the solid is real. We had confused concreteness with solidity. We now know that solidity is itself secondary and not primary. Physical reality, including the most obdurate objects, is composed of wave patterns, vibrations, energy events, electronic happenings. The excessive abstractness of the materialist view of physical reality lies partly in its unawareness of the dynamic constituency of even the most stationary solid object. Beneath the flow of life and even the placid facade of the Rocky Mountains there lies a story of process. It is a story in which the energy events that compose natural phenomena have engaged themselves in a dance of becoming and perishing, inheriting and "feeling" each other for millions of years. It is this process, and not some imaginary impermeable particles or inert stuff, that gives rise to the rocks as well as to life and mind. All physical objects are composed of patterns of process. If we try to imagine that there must be something solid beneath the process, then this is because we are still being tricked by the assumptions of common sense and classical physics upon which materialism rests.

As Bergson taught us half a century ago, we need not look beyond our own personal experience to have sufficient evidence of the utterly processive nature of reality.

> Our personality, which is being built up each instant with its accumulated experience, changes without ceasing. By changing, it prevents any state, although superficially identical with another, from ever repeating it in its very depth. That is why our duration is irreversible. . . .
>
> . . .
>
> Thus our personality shoots, grows and ripens without ceasing. Each of its moments is something new added to what was before.[5]

But, as the Buddha also taught, there is something about us that has an aversion to the perpetual perishing of each "now." We have a tendency to cling to the present or the past, the same tendency that leads to the illusion that there is a final solidity to things. It is a tendency analogous to the one portrayed by Sartre, whereby we flee from our freedom into the deterministic world of objects. We do not easily accept the idea of a world in process, partly because process entails perishability.

The flow of our own personalities through time cannot be divorced from the general context of the universe on which their becoming is borne. Bergson was himself dualistic in his divorcing mind and life from matter. But he was correct in his situating our own becoming in the stream of a universal becoming. Whitehead has radicalized this insight of Bergson's and has eliminated any dualism. He has emphasized the continuity between our own becoming and that of physical reality. We are in utter continuity with the processive universe.

If we take this continuity seriously then we must abolish the dualistic tendency to read our mental activity as though it were not also part of the inner essence of nature. Scientific thought, under the impact of dualism, has simply assumed that mental occurrences are not part of the cosmic arena, that mentality and nature belong to completely different realms. However, as Whitehead emphasizes:

> ... this sharp division between mentality and nature has no ground in our fundamental observation. We find ourselves living within nature. ... We should conceive mental operations as among the factors which make up the constitution of nature.[6]

I suspect that most of us have been so influenced by dualism that we find it quite difficult to think of our mental activity as part of the occurrences that make up nature. We somehow feel that our minds are outside of nature. And this feeling of mental exile is understandable as long as we conceive of nature itself as mindless. But it is precisely this assumption of the intrinsic mindlessness of nature that Whitehead asks us to question. Any absolutely clear line of demarcation that segregates our mental functioning from its cosmic matrix is purely arbitrary— indeed an illusion, a vestige of dualistic mythology.

Scientific materialism itself denies that there are any arbitrary breaks in nature. Everything is on a continuum with everything else. Everything that exists is explicable in terms of the mass-energy plenum. Our mental processes are also in principle fully explicable in terms of matter and energy. Seemingly, therefore, materialists are monists, since for them reality is reducible to the one realm of the physical. They apparently reject any dualism that would give to mind a separate ontological status. However, although they are monists metaphysically speaking, in that they reduce reality to only one kind of stuff, they remain dualists in their epistemology, that is, in their view of knowledge. They demand that we be objective in our understanding of nature, and this objectivity requires that we keep our subjectivity detached from the object, nature. The scientist's own mind must remain at a distance from the object being investigated in order that an "objective" perspective become possible. This divorce of the scientific subject's mind from the object being examined amounts to an epistemological dualism.

The attempt by materialists to hold together a metaphysical monism of matter with an epistemological dualism of mind over against matter seems to be incoherent. For on the one hand the materialist philosophy asserts that beings with minds evolved out of the cosmic process and, therefore, are continuous with nature. But on the other hand the same philosophy maintains that the minds of these beings are separate from the natural world during any valid act of knowing. It is very difficult to piece these contradictories together from the point of view of logic. Furthermore, materialism's epistemological dualism leaves open the door for the "existential" alienation of the subject from its cosmic context. It establishes a way of thinking that eventuates in the sense, expressed earlier by Klemke, that I am a stranger in an indifferent and hostile universe. The epistemological dualism implicit in scientific materialism inevitably leads to the feeling that nature is without purpose and that my own conscious life lacks any grounding in the universe.

The consensus of much recent thought, however, a great deal of it coming from physicists themselves, is that mind is intrinsic rather than extrinsic to nature. The universe is permeated not only with process but also with mentality. As in the ancient mythic visions, our own minds actually *belong* in the context of the cosmos.[7]

Physicist David Bohm, who dares to speculate on what he considers to be the philosophical implications of modern physics, asks whether thought itself might not be part of reality as a whole. He challenges us to ask: ". . . how are we to think coherently of a single, unbroken, flowing actuality of existence as a whole, containing both thought (consciousness) and external reality as we experience it?"[8]

> . . . to meet the challenge before us our notions of cosmology and of the general nature of reality must have room in them to permit a consistent account of consciousness. Vice versa, our notions of consciousness must have room in them to understand what it means for its content to be 'reality as a whole.' The two sets of notions together should then be such

as to allow for an understanding of how reality and consciousness are related.[9]

Relativity theory and quantum physics in the present century have given rise to a great deal of speculation like that of Bohm's. Much of this speculation has concluded that the scientific observer is not a detached spectator dualistically split off from nature. Rather the observer is really a participant whose mental activity cannot be separated from, and indeed inevitably intersects with, the objects being investigated. Physics itself seems to have blurred the line drawn by dualism between subject and object.

A more philosophical way to vanquish the dualism of mind and nature is to see them both as aspects of a unified cosmic process in which all the components of becoming are "mental." According to Whitehead something analogous to what we experience as mentality, something like "feeling" or "perception," is present throughout the natural world, not just in man, animals and plants, but also in the most fundamental constituents of the physical world. There is a "subjective" aspect to all "actual entities."[10]

Now it will no doubt seem to the reader who is unfamiliar with Whiteheadian thought that perceptivity, experience and mentality may be aspects of human and to some extent biological phenomena in general, but what about inanimate nature? Is it legitimate to hold, as we are doing here, that mentality is pervasive throughout the universe? Or is it not much more sensible to assume that mentality appears only very late and very locally in the evolutionary story? This may be granted if we are talking about mentality in the mode of human consciousness. Certainly consciousness does not exist at the level of atoms and electrons, nor does reflective self-awareness seem to appear in evolution until the human species comes onto the scene. But there is good reason for holding that mentality in the form of some sort of rudimentary "feeling" may be present at the level of the energy-events that give rise to electrons and atoms. For if our minds are continuous with the rest of nature (as even materialists acknowledge in their monistic metaphysics), then in some sense mentality is already present in the very stuff of the universe from which we have evolved. If we place matter and man on a continuum, one very fruitful way to understand ourselves is to do so as far as possible by specifying our material make-up. But it is also possible to understand a great deal about the nature of physical reality by beginning from the other end of the continuum. Since matter and mind are, after all, on the same unbroken spectrum, we may understand each partially in terms of the other. For this reason an understanding of mentality and its activity is not superfluous to our understanding of the whole universe.[11]

It is possible to understand a great deal about mind by analyzing it in terms of its molecular basis. It is also possible to reach a more concrete understanding of physical reality by recognizing its mental aspects. But how can we maintain something so apparently anthropomorphic? For at the very least mentality is by nature an experiential occurrence. And experience begins with feeling. When we say that the universe is mental, that it is composed of moments of feeling, it obviously appears as though we are projecting our own human experience onto something which is non-experiential. Is this not an instance of the "pathetic fallacy"?

In response, we must first re-emphasize that we are using the terms mentality, feeling, experience, and perceptivity in an *analogous* sense. Something *like* what we call feeling, perceiving, remembering, desiring, anticipating, liking and disliking must characterize every constituent aspect of reality. This does not necessarily mean that rocks have feelings. Rather it means that all objects, including inanimate ones, are composed of moments or occasions which have feeling as a constituent aspect of their actuality. The world of process is made up of units of becoming whose very essence is *feeling*. As Charles Hartshorne has suggested, it may be that feeling of feeling is an "... ultimate principle, applicable to deity and every other singular actuality."[12]

Science, of course, is unable by itself to penetrate the inner privacy or "subjectivity" of the moments of feeling that make up reality. Science always remains outside in its abstracting from the interiority of nature's constituent occasions of experience. And for that reason our terminology will inevitably sound foreign to those attuned to a scientific idiom. Therefore, it will strain our credulity at first to be told that the most concrete things in nature are not dead, inert, mindless. But how else would our world hang together as a *universe* unless things have a feeling for one another? To posit a subjective capacity to feel at the heart of all the moments that make up the cosmic process goes beyond the limits of scientific ways of thinking, but it is not a position that in any way conflicts with a coherent cosmology. Science, after all, usually deals with aggregates rather than with the fundamental units of reality of which I am speaking. And it is true, of course, that *aggregates* made up of concrete moments of feeling exhibit macroscopically inert qualities. A rock for example may legitimately be called inanimate and mindless. But the ultimate components of rocks or grains of sand or molecules and atoms are series of occurrences bound together by a feeling for one another. These series of occasions of experience (as Whitehead calls them) build up into patterns which give the outward appearance to our dull senses of firmness and immobility. With our senses we are not able to perceive directly the dynamic dance of mutual feeling that constitutes the foundation of the apparent stability of things. But it is reasonable to infer from the fact of nature's intrinsic continuity with our own mental experience that there must be at least a rudimentary type of feeling that binds all things to one another. What better word than "feeling" can we employ to indicate the power of attraction that binds the multiplicity of occasions into the organic unity of a universe?

Modern physics supports us in our proposal that the constituents of nature are not the lifeless particles that we tend to imagine as tiny versions of inert chunks of matter. The world of submicroscopic physics is so utterly different from the one that we observe in our ordinary experience that words and pictures fail us when we try to imagine what it is like in its inner constituency. If our suggestion sounds strange that this world of the infinitesimal is made up of feelings, then this is no stranger than any other proposals as to how to understand it.

In fact, though, there are very good positive reasons to make our own experiencing the central model for understanding the physical world. If this seems like the pathetic fallacy, then, Hartshorne says, it is less abstract than the "prosaic fallacy" of materialist monism.[13]

Perhaps we can grasp more clearly why we may attribute mentality to physical reality if we reflect more deeply upon our own feeling of transition within the cosmic process. One of the most immediately obvious aspects of our experience is the sense of becoming. In fact it is so obvious that we seldom explicitly advert to it. But if we reflect upon it now, and at the same time remember our continuity with the cosmic process, we will be able to clarify not only our own experience, but also essential aspects of the cosmos itself.

Each moment of our lives is made up of becoming and perishing. Each moment is a "throb of experience"[14] that comes into being, experiences a certain type of "enjoyment," and then perishes. Our personal lives are made up of a series of such becomings, enjoyments and perishings. As each moment perishes, however, it does not vanish into total oblivion. Instead it is taken up, as past experience, into the present moment of feeling. It is preserved in a component of present experience that we call memory. By virtue of this memory the past causally influences our present. And we may infer that this is how "efficient causation" occurs, not only in our own experience, but also throughout cosmic reality. It is the capacity of each present moment to receive the perished occasions of past experience into itself that allows the past to act causally upon the present. Were the present moment totally incapable of receiving into itself the deposit of past experiences, this past could exercise no influence upon it.

At the same time that our present experience is feeling the past it is also oriented toward the future. If we reflect carefully upon our present experience we realize that it is colored affectively by the future we have imagined for ourselves. The shape of what we consider to be our future possibilities tends to shade the quality of our present experience and to influence the manner in which we appropriate the data from our past. The ingression of the anticipated future into the present moment helps to constitute it precisely as this present moment. For example, my own writing of this present paragraph is colored by my anticipation of your reading it eventually. And this anticipation in turn governs what material my memory selects to write down.

Thus each moment of "feeling" has a polar quality to it. One pole, that of memory, reaches out and pulls in the past in a selectively qualifying manner. The other pole, that of anticipation, reaches out into the realm of possibilities and selectively qualifies the present moment's mode of feeling. Each perishable occasion of our experience, therefore, is composed of memory - enjoyment - anticipation.[15]

All of this may seem quite obvious to anyone who pauses to reflect on our humanly "mental" existence. What may not seem so obvious, however, is our suggestion that cosmic reality is in general composed of analogous types of occasions of experience. But once we eschew dualism and accept the continuity of nature and mentality such a conclusion is not out of order. Nature too may be pictured as made up of moments of memory - enjoyment - anticipation. There is nothing projective about this image. It would be projective only if mentality were not an intrinsic part of the cosmos. But there is no warrant for such a view.

This is not to suggest, of course, that sub-human occasions of feeling are as vivid and intense as are human feelings. Yet we may infer that such occasions possess at least a rudimentary kind of feeling. In an electron, for example, the moments of memory, enjoyment and anticipation would not add up to "consciousness," but they would at least count as a mode of "mentality," in our extended sense of the term. Our own conscious experience would then be a high-grade version of the mentality which constitutes all of reality.[16]

From the point of view of the questions we are discussing in this book there are important advantages in emphasizing the continuity of mind and nature. Charles Hartshorne has written extensively about the merits of this philosophical position, and a loose adaptation of his ideas on its advantages may be set forth in the following short list:[17]

1. The mentalist view overcomes the false problem of how matter gives rise to life and mind. Instead the real problem is how higher types of mind developed out of lower types.

2. The mentalist view does justice to the scientific intuition that there is a certain kind of continuity between matter and life.

3. It provides a basis for understanding the relationship of mind to body.

4. It allows us to see secondary qualities as intrinsic aspects of nature rather than the projections of subjectivity that materialism understands them to be.

5. Perhaps most important of all, the pervasive presence of mind in nature provides a receptive basis for a teleological influence that can be felt by all of the component occasions of experience.

6. Finally, the philosophy of mind-in-nature provides the basis for our rethinking the notion of perception.

To this latter issue we shall now turn.

Perception

If we situate mind inside of nature then we must revise our whole notion of perception. In doing so, we will be able to provide a new basis for discussion of the relationship of science to religion and of the issue of nature and purpose. Much of this discussion will be taken up in the final two chapters, but a brief introduction to Whitehead's highly original discussion of perception is appropriate at this point.[18]

Usually when we talk of perception we are thinking of sense-perception, what we experience by taste, sight, touch, hearing, smelling. And we also usually assume that it is through the five senses that we make our first and most fundamental contact with the world outside our minds. Again, this notion of perception is intimately tied up with dualism. It assumes that there is a mind separated off from the world, and that the senses bring material from the world outside into the mind. Although this notion of perception has been the dominant epistemological view in modern philosophy, it has never adequately explained precisely how the outside world and the mediating senses get over to the (totally different) realm of mind. There is always the suggestion that "somehow" the transition from matter to mind is made. But it is never specified exactly how.

By envisaging nature as pervasively perceptive we can offer a solution to this problem. Nature is made up of moments of perception. But what is perceived by these moments of perception? The Whiteheadian reply is that each "occasion of experience" perceives, synthesizes into its own "feeling" the immediately preceding moment. That preceding occasion had become, momentarily endured, and then perished. As it perished, however, it became the "material" to be synthesized in the present moment of perception. And the present moment, after perishing, will become the objective datum to be perceived in the "memory" of a subsequent occasion. Each perished occasion is felt or "remembered" in a distinctive way by subsequent occasions. Perception, then, is really a form of memory, and our own experience of remembering is perhaps the best way to understand what Whitehead means by perception.[19]

One of the most noteworthy features of our memory is that some items we recall are much more vivid than others. The immediate past is much more so than experiences of long ago. And it may be extremely difficult to bring back temporally distant experiences with any degree of clarity. Nonetheless, those remote experiences are still at least a dim part of our memory, and they surely exercise a causal efficacy on our existence here and now (as depth psychology has documented). In memory we receive the past into our present experience in different degrees of distinctness, and sometimes the indistinct remote past is more powerfully influential on our present feeling than is the distinct immediate past. It has an "importance" that the immediate past perhaps does not.

So it is with perception as Whitehead understands it. When we perceive something we are in fact remembering the perished and past moments of experience that are being taken into the present moment of feeling. Usually what stands out most vividly in our feeling is the immediate past, and this immediate past constitutes the data of sense perception. Here the past is so immediate that, as it were, it melts into the present. But our perception takes into itself the accumulated experiences of the remote and obscure past as well. And this past includes not only our own personal experiences. Since we are organically tied into the cosmos, there is a sense in which all of the experiences that have made up the universe enter vaguely, but efficaciously, into our experience also. Whitehead refers to this vague but significant experience as perception in the mode of causal efficacy. And he calls our experience of the contemporary world, behind which there lurks the deposit of accumulated past experience, perception in the mode of presentational immediacy. (For the sake of simplicity I shall call these respectively "primary" and "secondary" perception.) As we proceed we shall be able to draw some important implications for our topic from this initially troubling but philosophically illuminating distinction of two kinds of perception.

I earlier stated that all occasions of experience, being analogous to our own, have in association with their feelings the aspects of "remembering," "enjoying" and "anticipating." This extension of their perceptivity not only toward the past but also toward the future guarantees the uniqueness of each of these moments. Whitehead even uses the term "de-cision" to characterize how each moment "cuts itself off" from some anticipations and memories in order "decisively" to pattern its feeling (enjoyment) in a definite way.[20] Each moment is thus made up of a unique feeling tone composed of a distinctive "memory" and "anticipation."

It is characteristic of this view that each moment of experience is perceptive not only of the immediate past of the universe, but, in a vague way, of the entire past set of occurrences that have constituted the world process. This view also fits that described by modern physicists. The fields of force that make up the world all mutually interpenetrate, all influence each other, however faintly. The forces in the furthest stars are not unrelated to the electronic events occurring in my brain. This is a rather poetic view, but one justified by modern physics. Whitehead contrasts this modern view with the classical one upon which materialism is based. In the universe of classical physics, he says,

> ... the concept of matter presupposed simple location. Each bit of matter was self-contained, localized in a region with a passive, static network of spatial relations, entwined in a uniform relational system from infinity to infinity and from eternity to eternity. But in the modern concept the group of agitations which we term matter is fused into its environment. There is no possibility of a detached, self-contained local existence. The environment enters into the nature of each thing. ... In truth, the notion of the self-contained particle of matter, self-sufficient within its local habitation, is an abstraction.[21]

And correspondingly, "any local agitation shakes the whole universe."[22]

What renders possible this mutual interpretation of events postulated by quantum physics is that the concrete constituents of nature are all perceptive by nature. They are actually constituted by their capacity to feel. Each moment of perception, then, may be imagined as experiencing the whole universe vaguely and a certain proximate sector of it more vividly. That is, perception is a process of refining and "clarifying" the misty experience of the whole into the enjoyment of a unique and definite feeling.

Our own perception of the universe at the level of consciousness shares the polar quality that pertains to all perception. What we call sense perception is a rather late and somewhat abstract version of a much more global feeling we have, at a visceral level, of the entire universe entering into our experience. If the physicist is correct that the whole universe is in a sense everywhere, then our own experience is not exempt from such a remarkable state of affairs. Our own perceptivity feels in a cloudy way the entire universe. And our sense perception cuts off a thin slice of this global content and presents it to us with a certain vividness lacking in our global perception.

If we understand "perception" only as "sense-perception," then I would suggest that this view is too narrow. For prior to the clear and distinct impressions of the world given to us through our five senses we have already experienced the world's entering into our being and becoming in a much more fundamental way. For the sake of simplicity I shall call this experience "primary perception," and I shall distinguish it from "secondary perception" which is that of the five senses. In relation to primary perception the data of sense perception are rather late and abstract refinements of the material that is felt in our primary experience of the world.

Perception may be understood, therefore, as a process moving from the pole of primary perception to that of sense perception. At the primary pole of the perceptive process there is a vague and undefined feeling of the influence of the world on our being and becoming. Here the universe is felt as continuous with and "grounding" the perceiver's own existence. At this pole of perception there is no clear and distinct impression of things. Primary perception is vague, unclear, indistinct. For this reason we seldom advert to it, and most philosophers fail even to acknowledge its presence, even though it is causal of our very existence. We know about it more through philosophical inference and through drawing out important implications from recent physics than by way of direct experience. The content given to us at this global pole of feeling can never be brought fully to expression. I shall propose in Chapter 11 that it is the nature of *symbolic* expression to represent to us some aspects of what we receive in primary perception.[23] And for this reason we must not be overly critical of the apparently fuzzy and ambiguous character of symbolic representation. We should instead anticipate that if all reality is somehow ingredient in our experience at the pole of primary perception, no particular expression could fully retrieve it, and different peoples will represent their primary perception in radically different ways, depending on cultural and historical conditions. I shall later employ this notion of primary perception as a basis for understanding how religion relates to our experience and to science.

Conclusion

What are the implications of this vision of mind in nature for the question of purpose in the universe? If the universe is in any sense globally purposive, then mentality would have to be a pervasive and not merely a localized, fragmentary aspect of it. To be able to receive the impregnation of universal purpose, should there be such, the cosmos would have to possess an intrinsic receptivity to it. The constituent aspects of the universe must be units of feeling open to receive new possibilities of patterning. In this chapter I have proposed a notion of physical reality that is pervasively perceptive. At its base nature is made up of feeling-events composed of memory, enjoyment and anticipation. Through their memory the feelings allow the past to have a causal impact on the present. And through both the memory and the anticipatory pole of these units of feeling a cosmic aim or purpose may be envisaged as insinuating itself into the interior workings of the universe. In Chapter 8 I shall develop this possibility in more detail.

4.

Matter and Life

One of the striking ironies of our age is that while physics, formerly the "hardest" science, is becoming increasingly less materialistic, biology (and to some extent physiology and brain science) are now the strongholds of materialism in science. While the notion of matter has been progressively "dematerialized" by quantum and relativity physics, the life sciences still cling to a rather Newtonian concept of the physical. Whereas the dichotomy of subject and object has been challenged by experiments in modern physics, a Cartesian dualism still provides the philosophical background of modern molecular biology and, more recently, sociobiology. At a time when the physical sciences have dissolved the atoms of Democritus, the particles of Newton and the mechanisms of Descartes into downy abstractions, biology has become more and more atomistic and mechanistic. And, finally, as the notion of "field" has assumed primacy in the explanation of physical phenomena, it is only rarely employed in biological and neurophysiological theory. The sciences that deal explicitly with life and mind are more materialistic than those that deal directly with the physical universe.

In the previous chapter I proposed an alternative to the notion of physical reality espoused by scientific materialism. My proposal was heavily influenced by ideas of Whitehead and Hartshorne. In the present chapter I shall utilize the thought especially of Michael Polanyi to challenge the kind of materialism that dominates the life sciences. I shall be discussing primarily the contemporary attempts to reduce life and mind to "matter" as it is understood by a physics and chemistry that may themselves be out of date. I shall argue here that though the temptation to reduce life and mind to "matter" is quite understandable today given the amazing advances of molecular biology and brain science, it is, nevertheless, a temptation that must be avoided in the name of simple logic.

Francis Crick, one of the pioneers in molecular biology, wrote in his widely read book, *Of Molecules and Men*:

> The ultimate aim of the modern movement in biology is in fact to explain *all* biology in terms of physics and chemistry. (Emphasis original)[1]

And Crick's colleague, James Watson, was convinced that not only genetic but other aspects of life as well are reducible to explanation at the molecular level:

> Complete certainty exists among essentially all biochemists that the other characteristics of living organisms (for example, selective permeability across all membranes, muscle contraction, and the hearing and memory process) will all be completely understood in terms of the coordinative interactions of large and small molecules.[2]

This opinion is echoed in numerous scientific essays today. Richard Dawkins, in his celebrated book, *The Selfish Gene*, exemplifies the same position.[3] And a similar reduction of biology to a molecular science may be found in the writings of E.O. Wilson, Ernst Mayr, Jacques Monod and numerous other highly respected scientific writers.[4] In *Chance and Necessity*, for example, Monod gives one of the most forceful renditions of the view that biochemical analysis is "obviously" the sole avenue to understanding the secret of life.[5] Decades ago Jacques Loeb had already set forth the program of inquiry still emulated today by many biologists:

> Living organisms are chemical machines consisting chiefly of colloidal material and possessing the peculiarity of pre-

serving and reproducing themselves. . . . The essential difference between living and non-living matter consists in this:
the living cell synthesizes its own complicated specific material from indifferent or non-specific simple compounds of the
surrounding medium, while the crystal simply adds the molecules found in its supersaturated solution. This synthetic
power of transforming small "building stones" into the complicated compounds specific for each organism is the "secret
of life" or rather one of the secrets of life.[6]

If this removal of the boundaries between the life sciences
and the physical sciences is not the conventional wisdom among
biologists today, then it is at least a sufficiently influential
position to deserve closer examination.

Needless to say, many biologists are uncomfortable with
the stark reduction of their discipline to what are often considered "lower" and "harder" sciences. Yet they are not often able
to clarify conceptually why biology should be given the status
of an autonomous science. In this chapter I shall urge them not
to give up their persistence in clinging to the distinctiveness of
their field of inquiry in spite of the apparent inroads made into
it by the physical sciences. There are good logical, and not
merely psychological, reasons for their stubbornness.

It might not be immediately obvious, though, how our
discussion of the question of biology's independence relates to
the general theme of this book. How does the apparently innoc-
uous question "Is biology reducible to chemistry and physics?"
fit into the whole issue of whether the universe is in any sense a
purposeful one?

In response, let us momentarily suppose, with the teleologi-
cally biased traditions of religious and philosophical wisdom
(the so-called "perennial philosophy"), that the universe is a
hierarchy of "levels," or "dimensions" (or "fields" of influence,
if we wish to employ a more contemporary metaphor). For the
sake of convenience I shall use the more traditional term "levels" in my discussion even though I have serious reservations
about doing so. The vertical imagery associated with the idea of

a hierarchy of levels can be quite misleading. However, since the reader by now has learned to "mistrust simplicity," I may assume that he or she will at least first allow me to seek it.

In any case, traditional thought pictures the universe as a hierarchy of levels. These levels are, in ascending order, the material, the living, the conscious and the transcendent: matter, life, mind and God (or however the ultimate is named). In this cosmography life processes transcend material ones, mental processes transcend living ones, and the divine transcends the totality giving purpose and order to it. In this picture there is an ontological discontinuity as we move from one level to the next. There is an intuition that some factor is present at the level of life that is not present at the level of matter, and that there is a qualitative difference distinguishing mind from life, and so on. The traditional academic division of disciplines is governed by this sense of ontological discontinuity, and so biology departments have been separated administratively from those of chemistry and physics.

Today, however, a serious question has arisen as to whether there is any logical justification for this division. And where custom dictates that for the sake of convenience we keep to the traditional academic structure, the philosophical question still remains as to whether biology (or psychology or any other human science) has a genuine right to autonomous existence.

The reasons for this suspicion are clear. The obvious physical continuity of atomic and molecular make-up that runs from the level of rocks to that of brains compels us to wonder whether it is still feasible to cling to the intuition of ontological discontinuity. Something in us still insinuates that there is a world of difference between a rock and a frog, but molecular biology and neurophysiology see only chains of atoms everywhere. In the face of this physical continuity that cuts across the traditional lines of demarcation and alleged qualitative leaps in the hierarchy, can we still logically hold to the sense of ontological discontinuity?

Our discussion of the question of biology's reducibility to the physical sciences is, therefore, a kind of test case. It is a question which holds the key to whether the entire hierarchy should or should not be collapsed to the level of matter. It therefore bears directly on the issue of purpose in nature.

I think it is highly questionable whether a complete dismantling of the hierarchy can be consistently and logically executed. I agree with Polanyi that it is possible to hold together the fact of physical continuity with the hierarchical conception of ontological discontinuity. And a discussion of biological reductionism may be our best access to formulating a defense of the hierarchical view as well as some version of the teleological vision of the cosmos.

However, before undertaking any such defense of the notion of ontological discontinuity today we must acknowledge that the traditional hierarchy has to be considerably modified in the light of modern science. In the first place evolutionary theory demands that we unleash the hierarchy from its rigid verticality. The emergence of life comes chronologically billions of years after the birth of matter. And the appearance of mind (in the sense of *consciousness*, not in the sense of the pervasive mentality that constitutes all actualities) is a relatively recent development in our corner of the universe at least. To the materialist the late, apparently accidental, precarious and localized entry of life and consciousness onto our planet fortifies the view of physical continuity. Consequently we must take this "historical continuity" into account if we are still to affirm an ontological discontinuity. We must ask whether the physical and historical continuity that evolutionary theory posits, in its picture of life and consciousness arising from a soup of chemicals, rubs out the hierarchical distinction of levels.[7]

In the second place the traditional hierarchy may have to be altered to fit the "general systems" view of physical reality according to which there are countless levels of organization in physical reality and correspondingly numerous leaps and qualitative distinctions throughout the universe. General systems theory sees autonomy in biology but also recognizes discontinuity in prebiotic patterns of organization. In a sense there is just as much discontinuity of patterning between an electron and an atom or an atom and a molecule as there is between a molecule and a living cell. The leap from matter to life is only one of many leaps in nature's evolution.[8]

In the third place we must keep in mind the proposal made earlier that beneath the physical continuity of nature there is a deeper processive continuity that is perceptive or "mental." What we normally take as physical reality is composed of a continuous, dynamic process of occasions of experience inheriting one another through a mode of activity that can best be called "feeling." This aspect of feeling is the deepest root of the continuity that binds all things together. In fact the point of view taken in this book is that the mutual continuity of all actualities is much deeper and more cohesive even than that postulated by materialists. The organic, sentient cohesiveness in all of nature, however, does not eliminate the possibility of qualitative leaps in the emergence of higher and more complex organismic arrangements.

In the fourth place we must fully acknowledge the recent discoveries pertaining to the chemistry underlying the life process. It is clear today that life does in fact have a molecular basis that can be specified by chemical analysis. The "secret" of life, growth and heredity seems to lie in the movement and combination of nucleic and amino acids. These acids in turn are merely complex chains of atoms (carbon, hydrogen, oxygen, nitrogen). It is little wonder, therefore, that some scientific thinkers would be tempted to the view that life is reducible to a molecular basis.

The most important molecule involved in living things is called DNA. The DNA molecule, made up of four types of nucleic acids (signified by the letters A, C, T and G) constitutes a code, of which the four nucleic acids in various triadic arrangements are the alphabet. The manner in which the letters of this code are patterned determines the way in which the proteins of an organism (composed of amino acids) will be structured. Through a messenger and transfer process involving a group of acids called RNA, the genetic code inscribed in the DNA molecule will give rise to determinate living beings such as bacteria, mice or humans. The whole process seems utterly physical and chemical. Life appears to be not the result of miracle but rather of blind and impersonal material laws.

By using the language of chemistry modern biology has also given us an updated version of Darwin's theory of evolution. Occasionally, according to the neo-Darwinist, the chain of nucleic acids in DNA undergoes an accidental modification. A portion of the chain is perhaps eliminated, inverted, or repositioned. This modification is called a mutation, and it is apparently the result of blind chance. The result is that in the translation process the proteins of the coded organism will be restructured according to the mutated DNA. If this restructuring is advantageous, nature selects the organism for survival; if the restructuring enfeebles the organism, as happens with most mutations, the outcome may be extinction. The organisms selected by nature for survival will pass on to their offspring the favorable genetic characteristics. And in this fashion new species periodically come into existence.

The DNA molecule is for the most part very stable and conservative. But occasionally the pull of entropy, a cosmic ray or some other (unknown) factor will bring about a mutation in the genetic code. This miniscule chemical aberration may cause a large or small change in the encoded organism. Then nature selects those mutated organisms which can accommodate themselves most readily to a particular environment. Eventually, as a result of chance mutations in DNA, accidental modifications subjected to the pressure of natural selection, there emerge the "higher" animals and, at last, man.

According to many biologists today this chemical explanation of life and evolution has no need to resort to the idea of purpose or to what Aristotle termed final cause. In other words modern biology has no use for "teleological" explanations. Mechanical-chemical explanations are sufficient. As Wilson says:

> . . . no species, ours included, possesses a purpose beyond the imperatives created by its genetic history. Species may have vast potential for guidance and mental process but they lack

any imminent [*sic*] purpose or guidance from agents beyond their immediate environment or even an evolutionary goal toward which their molecular architecture automatically steers them.[9]

And Richard Dawkins adds a Darwinian emphasis:

Darwin's theory of evolution by natural selection is satisfying because it shows us a way in which simplicity could change into complexity, how unordered atoms could group themselves into ever more complex patterns until they ended up manufacturing people. Darwin provides a solution, the only feasible one so far suggested, to the deep problem of our existence.[10]

Dawkins begins his book, *The Selfish Gene*, with the question: Why do we exist? He tells us that Darwin's theory, brought up to date by modern molecular biology, provides the only sensible answer to this question. Thus chemistry (in the guise of genetics) is given the burden of answering the questions formerly reserved for seers, metaphysicians and theologians. Our four-level hierarchy has completely collapsed. Any considerations of teleology are deemed to be childish and intellectually obscurantist. We see in Dawkins, Wilson, Monod, and their many colleagues the implementation not only of Crick's proposal to reduce biology to the "harder" sciences, but also the hope of answering all questions—even metaphysical-religious ones such as "Why do I exist?"—in terms of the meandering of molecules, without any reference to final causal considerations. Therefore, our question whether biology is reducible to physics and chemistry is not as innocent as it may initially appear to be. It bears directly on the question of purpose in evolution.

The Irreducibility of Life[11]

It is doubtful, though, whether life can be decisively reduced to the level of matter. If it could, then chemistry (and physics) would be able, eventually at least, to provide an adequate explanation of it. We must ask, then, whether the science of chemistry can exhaustively explain what life is, even in principle. Most biologists would agree that chemistry has not yet sorted out all of the "mysteries" in the life process. But many of them cling to the expectation that it will do so progressively as our techniques of analysis become more advanced.

That such a hope may be destined for frustration lies in the simple fact that the DNA molecule essential for life functions primarily as a code. As even mechanistic biologists admit, the DNA molecule is a code capable of containing and transmitting *information*. It is instructive to dwell on these notions of code and information, for it is questionable whether chemistry is appropriate as a science to understand them adequately.

A code is a set of elements that can be arranged and rearranged so as to bear specific information. Our alphabet is a clear example of a code. Its twenty-six component letters can be maneuvered into an endless variety of patterns containing meaning or information. The information resides not in the letters themselves but in the specific sequence that is given to the letters in a piece of writing.

The same also may hold in the case of DNA. The letters of this code are nucleic acids (A, C, T and G) arranged sequentially in triadic formations. It is not the acids themselves that contain the information in DNA. Rather it is the *specific sequence* of base pairs that bears the "meaning." So we must ask whether chemistry (or any physical science) can specify the overall sequence of nucleic acids that determines the kinds and shapes of organisms existing in the biosphere.

With Polanyi I shall argue that the sequence of base pairs in DNA is in fact *extraneous* to the chemistry underlying the life process.[12] Chemical activity is of course a necessary condition for the emergence and existence of life. But it is not a sufficient condition. Materialism founders on the logical confusion of necessary with sufficient conditions.

In order to clarify this point of logic an analogy may help. Letters appear on the page before you because there is a certain chemical property in ink that compels it to bond with paper. Without this deterministic, invariantly stable property you would see no letters and, therefore, would not be able to grasp what I am trying to communicate to you. Consequently, we may safely say that, in this context at least, chemical forces, operating impersonally, blindly, deterministically are a necessary condition for the transferral of information to you, the reader. But there is certainly more involved here than chemistry. The letters on the page before you have a very specific *sequence*. (*Sequence* is the most important term in our discussion in this chapter.) Does chemistry determine the sequence of letters on this page? Or is there not something *extraneous* to chemistry that gives the specific sequence? Again, chemical reactions or properties are a *necessary* condition for my communicating information, but are they a *sufficient* condition? Is not something else involved here?

It is clear that the meaning or information you are receiving now is primarily a result of the specific sequence of letters on this page and not of the chemistry of ink and paper. And while you the reader and I the writer are both *relying on* the workings of invariant chemical processes, the *meaning is extraneous to the chemistry*. You do not go to the chemist as such to discern the meaning of a chapter in this book. The meaning of this chapter has been made "incarnate" by the author in a *specific sequence of letters of a code* whose variability has allowed him to arrange them in the pattern you see before you. And while he is relying on the stability of chemical processes to inform you, he would no doubt be insulted if someone told him that an analysis of the chemistry of ink and paper would yield an adequate understanding of this chapter.[13]

Now are we sure that the case of DNA's information-bearing ability is completely different from this example? Granted, there are obvious disparities. Still is it not possible that the *specific sequence* of base-pairs in a DNA molecule is extraneous to the chemistry which bonds the nucleic acids to one another? I think the question is at least left open. Our analogy of letters on a page, derived from Michael Polanyi, makes us wonder whether we can dogmatically state that life is nothing but the result of chemical forces and that biology is reducible to chemistry and physics. Can we rule out the presence of some sort of "extraneous" causation operating somehow at the level of DNA's sequence, communicating "information" through the instability of the code, writing its meaning into the cosmos?[14]

But let us stop for we are getting outrageous. There is no *tangible* evidence of such an agency. We cannot locate any cosmic informer at the interstices of the loosened and readjusted acids in the DNA chain. Moreover, we know now the degree to which chance seems to enter into the evolutionary process. "Chance" appears to be the scribbler, eraser and communicator. How can we talk about extraneous agency without trailing off into mystification?

In this chapter I have taken only a small step toward a response to this question, but it may turn out to be an important one. I have tried to show that it is not altogether obvious that the sequence of base pairs in the DNA molecule is determined only by chemistry or that chemistry alone can illuminate this sequence. In other words, it is not clear that biology is a molecular science, reducible to chemistry and then to physics. I cannot prove that there is any extraneous causation at work, but in subsequent chapters I shall try at least to explain why it is that any such causation would not be accessible to our efforts at verification.

Conclusion

Marjorie Grene summarizes our critique of the reductivist project:

> What makes DNA do its work is not its chemistry but the order of the bases along the DNA chain. It is this order which is a code to be read out by the developing organism. The laws of physics and chemistry hold, as reductivists rightly insist, universally; they are entirely unaffected by the particular linear sequence that characterizes the triplet code. Any order is possible physico-chemically; therefore physics

and chemistry cannot specify *which* order will in fact succeed in functioning as a code.[15]

Is it not legitimate to go beyond the chemical factors involved and to ask what factors may be involved in determining the *specific sequence* in the code of life? Can the answer possibly be chance alone?

But let me be more positive. At times in the past the cosmos has been compared to a "teaching" or to a book. Throughout most of human history our universe has been viewed as a repository of meaning. It is not entirely out of the question that modern molecular biology is but one of several recent scientific developments that have made it possible for us to rehabilitate this intuition in a fresh way. It is in the order or sequence of the components of the cosmos that its meaning would reside. The specific sequence of vibrations gives an electron its character or an atom its properties. The specific sequence of nucleotides determines the various kinds of life that appear in evolution. Perhaps our universe is closer to an embodiment of "intelligence" than we have been accustomed to think. Science in the usual sense does not deal adequately with the factor of coded sequence; it does not often even advert to it, though the use of computer models is beginning to enhance our understanding of the many possible patterns of information at every level of matter and life. Generally, however, science formulates the laws binding one component to another without explicit consideration of the overall sequence of cosmic components or events. The reasons for this reticence will be discussed in the next chapter.

5.

Non-Energetic Causation and Cosmic Purpose

We have just looked at the view that biology is in principle reducible to physics and chemistry and that life can be fully explained in terms of the movements of molecules and atoms. The essence of Polanyi's critique of this view is that life requires something *extraneous* to physics and chemistry in order to have emerged in evolution. According to one of his analogies: just as the sequence of letters on a page is extraneous to the chemistry of ink and paper, so the sequence of nucleic acids in the DNA molecule (which, when translated, determines the shape of an organism and its specific characteristics) is extraneous to the chemical forces operative in the genetic process. Though life processes rely upon physico-chemical processes, Polanyi insists that they cannot be fully explained in terms of physics and chemistry. There are extraneous organizational factors at work in the emergence of life that cannot be specified by the more basic sciences. Therefore biology cannot be reduced to physics and chemistry.[1]

To many scientific thinkers, however, any talk about "extraneous" organizational principles operative in nature sounds somewhat mystical. Or it may also sound like a reversion to metaphysical dualism. Reference to non-physical causation does not resonate harmoniously with mechanistic biology which attempts to explain life in terms of specifiable chemical components and physical forces. The postulation of extraneous organizational principles leads biologists like Monod to classify

Polanyi's thought as vitalistic.[2] (Vitalism is the philosophy of nature which holds that the existence of life is exclusively the result of some extra-material principle totally different from matter.) An extraneous cause that cannot be grasped in terms of the laws governing mass and energy appears to abide outside the realm of legitimate scientific reference. It belongs to the domain of the mystical. Therefore it need not be taken seriously by scientific thought.

In this chapter I would like to argue that extraneous causation is a legitimate notion, that it is not a vitalistic ploy but instead an indispensable explanatory idea, though not one capable of scientific verification. In doing so I shall introduce some ideas of Rupert Sheldrake and place them alongside suggestions made by Polanyi. And finally I shall relate the contributions of both thinkers to the larger question of nature and purpose.

Sheldrake's Hypothesis of Formative Causation

Rupert Sheldrake has recently written a book which, I think, is destined to arouse much discussion and controversy. It is entitled *A New Science of Life,* and the important subtitle reads: "The Hypothesis of Formative Causation."[3] The book's thesis is that in addition to mechanical and energetic causation as understood by the conventional materialist approach of most biologists, a fuller grasp of the phenomena of matter, life and consciousness requires the hypothesis of "formative causation." None of the entities in nature can be explained fully in terms of the movement of molecules. This axiom applies especially, though not exclusively, to life forms. Some non-mechanical causative principle of order is required to explain, for example, why the molecules of living beings come together into specific shapes, why organisms develop specific characteristics or have the capacity to regulate their metabolism or readjust and reintegrate themselves holistically when injured or when challenged by their environment. Some formative cause which canalizes the process of growth and development has to be postulated to explain why animals develop reflexes, instincts, habits and behavior that give them their defining qualities. This canalization occurs through "morphogenetic fields." Going contrary to what he calls the orthodox approach of mechanistic biology, Sheldrake, like Polanyi, insists upon the necessity of an extraneous causal factor in addition to the mechanical and energetic causes operative in the biosphere. His book has obvious implications for the whole problem of nature and purpose.

I shall not attempt to summarize Sheldrake's hypothesis in detail. Much of it remains highly speculative, and I would not care to defend all of it. At times it is quite unconvincing. I am troubled, for example, by Sheldrake's expectation that the hypothesis of formative causation can be verified by scientific experimentation. I would maintain, rather, that the hypothesis is trivialized and misunderstood if it is placed in the category of the verifiable and falsifiable propositions of empirical science. Instead it has more plausibility as a metaphysical than as a scientific instrument of explanation. And it is as such that I shall explore its possibilities for illuminating the nature of the extraneous causal factors required in an emergent universe.

The most important and applicable aspect of Sheldrake's proposal, for our purposes, lies in his development of the notion of morphogenetic fields to explain the hierarchical structure of nature. Sheldrake is not the first to use this notion, but his presentation is one of the clearest to date, and I think it avoids the vitalistic overtones that have burdened other renditions of the idea.

"Morphogenesis" (from the Greek *morphe* = form, and *genesis* = birth, origin) means simply the process of something's coming-to-be according to a specific form. What, though, is meant by a morphogenetic "field"? The metaphor "field" is suggested by the effect that magnets or electromagnetic systems have on iron filings or other entities that are noncontiguous with the magnetic source. And the notion of gravitational "fields" exercising influence across space has long been a major aspect of modern science. In fact today the notion of "field" is often considered primary, while that of physical "body" is secondary to and derivative of field. After Einstein physical phenomena can no longer be explained in terms of energy alone: ". . . although energy can be regarded as the cause of change, the *ordering* of change depends on the spatial structure of the fields."[4] So there is a well-established precedent for use of the term "field" in scientific discourse.

A *morphogenetic* field, then, would be the non-energetic context of causation that accounts for the origin and development of physical and biological forms.[5]

Sheldrake takes up the suggestion made by some earlier biologists that there are morphogenetic fields exercising formative influence on the origin, epigenesis and activity of organisms. Such morphogenetic fields, however, are not confined to biological reality. They govern as well the formation of electrons, atoms, crystals and other inorganic systems.[6] Thus they do not enter as a kind of *deus ex machina* (in the manner depicted by some vitalists) only at the level of life. These causal fields are an essential and pervasive factor at every level in nature and evolution.

Precisely how these morphogenetic fields exercise their influence is a matter of speculation. Ordinary scientific procedures cannot specify how or where the formative causation of these fields intersects with physical phenomena.[7] For this reason the field theory has gained little acceptance among "orthodox" biologists. But Sheldrake is not put off by the fact of the apparently vaporous nature of morphogenetic fields. For mechanical explanation, especially in biology, simply cannot answer all the questions that arise concerning the origin, evolution and behavior of life. It is too much to expect that the morphological diversity and the organic versatility of organisms can be explained purely in terms of the bonding of chemicals. For example, the folding of a polypeptide chain into the three-dimensional structure of a protein seems to follow a specific form or pattern. Just as the flow of a stream is determined by a specific landscape, so it seems that the growth and development of the proteins follow an "epigenetic landscape" which is extraneous to the physico-chemical forces that energize the growth process.[8] And just as the geographical landscape is extraneous to the flow of water by the power of gravitation, so the epigenetic landscape is extraneous to the "flow" of energized matter operating by physico-chemical forces in the organism's epigenesis.

Thus it seems to Sheldrake that we need to posit a formative causation in addition to the mechanical causation involved in nature's structuration into specific kinds of entities. Things do end up with distinct shapes and characteristics. Can this morphological discreteness and diversity be accounted for only in mechanical-energetic terms? Though we cannot observe them directly, we must postulate also the existence of morphogenetic fields through which formative causation operates.[9] If fields are so determinative of the reality of electrons and stars, why should living beings be exempt from such influence also?

And yet it is baffling that these fields would be so elusive, so resistant to tangible grasp. Why does the idea of morphogenetic fields sound so suspiciously mystical? The reason is that these fields exercise their influence in a most unobtrusive manner. They are morphologically active while being energetically passive.[10] ". . . although morphogenetic fields can only bring about their effects in conjunction with energetic processes, they are not in themselves energetic."[11] Therefore, they are unavailable to the grasp of those scientific procedures which seek only to specify the mechanical-energetic factors in the production of effects.

> The idea of non-energetic formative causation is easier to grasp with the help of an architectural analogy. In order to construct a house, bricks and other building materials are necessary; so are the builders who put the materials into place; and so is the architectural plan which determines the form of the house. The same quantity of building materials could produce a house of different form on the basis of a different plan. Thus the plan can be regarded as a *cause* of the specific form of the house, although of course it is not the only cause: it could never be realized without the building materials and the activity of the builders. Similarly a specific morphogenetic field is a cause of the specific form taken up by a system, although it cannot act without suitable "building blocks" and without the energy necessary to move them into place.[12]

Sheldrake himself, however, does not think that these morphogenetic fields lie outside the scope of scientific methods of verification. Instead he speculates that they exercise their effects, not only in the realm of physics but also in biology, in a manner open to experimentation. He even suggests (in a way most scientists will inevitably find highly problematic) that experiments might be devised to verify the hypothesis of formative causation. It is here that I think he trivializes his metaphysical position by squeezing it into the too narrow framework of scientific inquiry. He concedes too much in the end to the methods of scientific materialism including the demand for tangible evidence. I would question whether we need to bring the hypothesis of formative causation before the court of scientific judgment, even if it does somehow find independent authentication there.

Sheldrake pictures morphogenetic fields as being the context in which forms (of life or physical reality) which arose in the past exercise their causal influence by a non-energetic "resonance" with subsequent similar systems.[13] Resonance of course is a physical analogy for something that is not physical: "A 'resonant' effect of form upon form across space and time would resemble energetic resonance in its selectivity, but it could not be accounted for in terms of any of the known types of resonance, nor would it involve a transmission of energy."[14] In order to distinguish it from energetic resonance, Sheldrake calls this process *morphic resonance*. Through this morphic resonance within a morphogenetic field the form of a past system can become present to a later similar system. ". . . the spatio-temporal pattern of the former *superimposes* itself on the latter."[15] "Morphic resonance takes place through morphogenetic fields and indeed gives rise to their characteristic structures. Not only does a specific morphogenetic field influence the form of a system . . . but also the form of this system influences the morphogenetic field and through it becomes present to subsequent systems."[16]

Since morphic resonance is non-energetic, and morphogenetic fields are not composed of mass or energy, there is no reason for us to expect them to have to obey the ordinary laws of physics. Morphic resonance can exercise its causal effect in a manner "unattenuated by time and space."[17] Therefore, a past system can exercise its influence across space and time from a distance, non-contiguously with its effects.

Interesting as this speculation may be, I doubt the need for Sheldrake to insist upon scientific experimentation in order to legitimate the hypothesis of formative causation. Such an "hypothesis" is a metaphysical necessity and not an *ad hoc* scientific exigency. Metaphysically speaking, in order for anything even to be, it must be ordered or patterned in some way.[18] Without some form it would be sheer indeterminate chaos. In other words it would be nothing. The form of something, as the ancient Greek philosophers recognized, is intrinsic to its very being. Everything, Aristotle taught, must have a "formal cause." Formative causation is a general aspect of all reality. Of course the Greeks do not have the final word on the subject, and we can possibly learn a lot from science about the results of morphogenetic causation. The merit of Sheldrake's book is that it boldly and intelligently speculates on the dynamic, epigenetic nature of morphogenesis in the biosphere. However, by specific experiments science can add little intensively to the legitimacy of the notion of formative causation (though it certainly may do so cumulatively). And I doubt seriously whether future scientific experimentation such as Sheldrake proposes will significantly add to or subtract from its viability.

After this qualification has been made, however, I think Sheldrake's presentation of the hypothesis of formative causation has a major contribution to make to discussion of the central issue in science and religion, namely, the question whether the fabric of nature is in any sense congruous with the religious hypothesis that the universe is purposeful. The manner in which divine purposiveness would exercise its influence on nature may be understood, in part at least, on the analogy of Sheldrake's notion of non-energetic morphogenetic causation.

Cosmic Purpose and Non-Energetic Causation

The scientific materialist usually attempts an explanation of phenomena exclusively in atomistic, molecular, macromolecular or genetic terms. Physico-chemical elements possess an empirical quality that can be expressed by way of pictures, models or mathematics. Its recondite nature, however, renders the idea of morphogenetic causation highly suspect. It appears simply too elusive to be given serious consideration by science as such. Morphogenetic fields have neither mass nor energy. And so to the materialist they do not seem to be part of the "real" world.

The absence of any direct empirical evidence of cosmic purpose is intricately linked with the lack of any immediately tangible evidence of morphogenetic fields that would exercise a causative influence on the formation of discrete systems in the natural world. It is nearly impossible for the mechanist to conceive, let alone imagine, how something which is energetically passive and void of mass can be nonetheless real and influential. Yet I would suggest that cosmic teleology (whatever its specific nature), as well as morphogenetic causation in general, would share this trait of concealment. Therefore, I shall attempt here by way of images and analogies to vindicate the possible reality of non-energetic causation. I would emphasize, however, that the following does not pretend to be a demonstration of the existence of morphogenetic fields or of cosmic purpose. Rather it attempts only to point out the logical and cosmological congruity of these unobtrusive formative factors with nature as understood by science.

Analogy "A"

Our first analogy is derived and adapted from one given by Michael Polanyi in *The Tacit Dimension*.[19] It concerns the way in which the laying of bricks in a town is influenced by the designs of the architect and, higher yet, the town-planner. To understand what a town is it is not sufficient to consult the brickmason. The latter of course can tell you a great deal about how bricks bond with one another and how their juxtaposition, one against or on top of another, contributes to the formation of a wall, a corner, a tower, etc. But this specification of the particulars of town-building does not really tell you what a town is. Nor does it give you all of the causal factors involved in its construction. For in addition to the "mechanical" causes specified by the mason there are "formative" causes provided by the architect's designs. These designs are themselves *energetically passive* and devoid of mass (except to the extent that they are portrayed by blue ink on white paper). And yet they exercise a causal influence without which there would be no town. They provide the pattern which gives the town its specific character. That is, they *cause* the town to be what it is, even though they do not possess the massiveness of a single brick. While the architect relies for the implementation of his plans upon the successful performance of the bricklayer, an analysis of the brick level does not tell us what is involved in the phenomenon of a town, except very superficially. For a wider understanding we need to consult the architect, and for a still more comprehensive vision we would have to be informed by the town-planner.

The feature of this analogy that I would like to draw out at this point is simply the fact that something need not be part of the mass-energy continuum in order to be causally real. Nor need it be energetically active in order to exercise influence. The formative designs of the architect are extraneous to the mechanically energetic bricklaying process, and yet they are profoundly influential. The purposes of the town planner are extraneous to the methods of architecture, and yet they are causal of the pattern that the architect's designs follow. There is a hierarchy of levels involved in building a town. And as we move up the hierarchy the levels become more subtle and less massive, though their causal importance increases. The town planner has more influence on the character of the town than does the architect, and the architect more than the bricklayer. Each level relies upon the lower, but cannot be exhaustively explained in terms of the lower. The higher has power to organize the lower levels even though it is less massive-energetic than those below it.

We may conclude from this example that the non-interference of formative causation is no argument against its existence and effectiveness. Our question, though, is whether something like this silent formative causation is operative in nature as a whole. Before returning to this question, let us look at another analogy.

Analogy "B"

This analogy is suggested by the manner in which a landscape causally shapes the structure and performance of a stream of water. Here the lay of the land in terms of hills and valleys, though energetically passive, determines the course a river will take, how large or small it will be at specific points, how fast or slow it will flow in particular regions, and how much physical potential or active energy it will have at various locations. Though non-energetic itself, the form of the landscape is a determinative factor in the amount of energy available in the river's flow. Formative causation, though itself non-energetic, is a factor in determining the kind and availability of energy. Passivity may in a certain sense be seen as prior to activity.

Now it is possible to study the flow of the river while prescinding altogether from the landscape. The landscape is a silent, unobtrusive horizon or background which is forgotten or suppressed as we focus on the energetic stream of water itself. The landscape's energetic passivity is not easily made the subject of explicit knowledge as long as we are focally concerned with the flow of water. And yet the energetic potential and activity of the stream is itself a gift of the landscape. The latter, as it were, recedes graciously into the background where its morphogenetic influence lies unacknowledged though quite real.

Again this is only an analogy. But we can make use of it to understand not only how specific systems of matter, life and consciousness arise, but also to symbolize the manner in which cosmic purpose may be operating graciously, silently, caringly in the universe.

Following this analogy I would see the mechanistic interpretation of matter, life and consciousness as so focused on the energetically causal flow of water (matter) that it suppresses any focal knowledge of the formative causation by the landscape (morphogenetic fields). In biological discussion when a few speculative biologists point to the necessity of an "epigenetic landscape" to make sense of embryogenesis, development and growth their colleagues usually summon them back to "reality" with sober accusations of mystification. Today there is very little entertainment among scientific thinkers of the possibility that the epigenesis of an organism is causally formed by a morphogenetic "landscape" in addition to the molecular movements of chemicals. It is almost as though the stream of water in our analogy were magically suspended independently of the landscape, and the specific contours which make it this particular stream have no relation to the lay of the land.

The Tao of Biology

What we have called "extraneous causation" is energetically passive and, therefore, unspecifiable by science, while remaining morphogenetically active. It may seem paradoxical that passivity gives rise to activity. But this is not the first place human thought has proposed such a paradox. The possibility of non-interfering effectiveness is a major intuition of one of the most revered and respected bodies of ancient wisdom, philosophical Taoism. Among the world's religious traditions there is perhaps none that bases itself so squarely on the principle of effective unobtrusiveness as Taoism. The Tao, the ultimate principle of reality, is said to exercise its influence on nature and man not by active causation but by *wu-wei*, an untranslatable term for "active inaction" or, as I would prefer, "effective non-interference" or "non-interfering effectiveness."

In the *Tao Te Ching*, a text attributed to Lao-Tzu (sixth century B.C.) the Tao (or "Way") that moves nature is symbolized as feminine, as like water, as like a valley, an uncarved block, or a child. All of these are seen as examples of *wu-wei*—they accomplish much while being passive, helpless, pliable. In Taoism the universe is governed by non-energetic causation. Common sense and physical science for the most part tend to notice only things which are prominent and forceful. Lao-Tzu, however, stresses the power of the negative, of that which does not stick out in obviousness. The Tao which shapes nature is so unprominent that one cannot even name it. It recedes behind or beyond all phenomena and is not to be found among the things which impress our senses. Yet it is all-powerful in its self-withdrawal. Tao is like water:

> That which is best is similar to water.
> Water profits ten thousand things and does not oppose them.
> It is always at rest in humble places that people dislike.
> Thus it is close to Tao. (Ch 8)[20]

The way of nature, according to Lao-Tzu, is non-interference. The area of our experience governed by force or active energy is superficial in comparison with the silent depth of the universe.

The Tao is not only non-interfering; it may even be spoken of as "non-being," in the sense that it does not fall among the class of things we normally refer to as "beings." Rather it is "no-thing." And precisely as such does it exercise its power. The *Tao Te Ching* gives these illustrative images:

> Thirty spokes are joined at the hub.
> From their non-being arises the function of the wheel.
> Lumps of clay are shaped into a vessel.
> From their non-being arises the functions of the vessel.
> Doors and windows are constructed together to make a
>   chamber.
> From their non-being arises the functions of the chamber.

Therefore, as individual beings, these things are useful
  materials.
Constructed together in their non-being, they give rise to
  function. (Ch 11)[21]

Wu Cheng (1249–1333) comments: "If it were not for the empty
space of the hub to turn round the wheel, there would be no
movement of the cart on the ground. If it were not for the
hollow space of the vessel to contain things, there would be no
space for storage. If it were not for the vacuity of the room
between the windows and doors for lights coming in and going
out, there would be no place to live."[22]

I would suggest that formative causation through morphogenetic fields makes itself felt at the levels of matter, life, mind
and the universe as a whole in this non-interfering manner of
influence. However, if there is universal purpose to cosmic
process, Taoism teaches us that we would be sensitive to it only
after we have ourselves learned the wisdom of *wu wei* and
allowed our lives to be formed accordingly. Scientific investiga-
tion, focusing on the spokes, the clay, the window and door
frames, is silenced when it comes to the void which makes
things functionally active. Awareness of cosmic purpose acting
non-energetically could occur only after a personal transforma-
tion in which the Taoist humility and sensitivity to non-being
has taken root.

In Christianity as well as other religious traditions besides
Taoism there is a fundamental conviction that "power is made
manifest in weakness." It is one of the central, but one of the
most disturbing, insights humans have had about the nature of
ultimate reality. Taoism expresses a conviction about the ultimate that is common to the mystical sense of many traditions:

Gaze at it; there is nothing to see.
It is called the formless.
Heed it; there is nothing to hear.
It is called the soundless.
Grasp it; there is nothing to hold on to.
It is called the immaterial.

> Invisible, it cannot be called by any name.
> It returns again to nothingness. (*Tao Te Ching* Ch 14)[23]

Somehow the power, the capacity to influence, resident in ultimate reality is not in spite of but rather a result of its non-availability. This intuition of Taoism (and I think of Christianity and other religious traditions also) makes somewhat pretentious the philosophical demand that all reality show itself phenomenally. The view that all reality should be within our grasp is, according to these traditions, a most impoverishing attitude rooted in a will to mastery. Both our senses and our minds need eventually to back off from the cloying obtrusiveness of things, objects, beings.

> Numerous colors make man sightless.
> Numerous sounds make man unable to hear.
> Numerous tastes make man tasteless. (*Tao Te Ching* Ch. 12)[24]

From the busy-ness of objects and sensations we need to be brought back to reality, to the undifferentiated fullness of Tao.

> Contemplate the ultimate void.
> Remain truly in quiescence.
> All things are together in action,
> But I look into their non-action. (*Tao Te Ching* Ch. 16)[25]

Scientific method is not equipped to deal with *wu wei* (non-action). For this reason the hypothesis of formative causation seems mystical. I suspect that it seems mystical because it is mystical. This is the reason for my objection to Sheldrake's attempt to bring formative causation into the focus of scientific objectification. Formative causation, acting non-energetically, must be respected for its Tao-like style of influence. It is not to be wondered at if scientific thinkers sense "mysticism" when they hear talk of extraneous causation. The hypothesis of formative causation is mystical (which is not the same as saying it is dualistic or vitalistic). Nor is it surprising that the hypothesis of extraneous formal causation would be subjected to the ridicule of scientific materialists. Such ridicule is not unanticipated, however:

> When a man of superior talent listens to Tao, he earnestly applies it.
> When an ordinary man listens to Tao, he seems to believe it and yet not to believe it.
> When the worst man listens to Tao, he greatly ridicules it.
> If he did not ridicule it,
>> it would not be the Tao. (Ch. 41)[26]

6.

Chance and God

Surely the question persists in spite of what we have argued in the previous chapter: Where is the *evidence* that an extraneous factor, a cause other than physical and chemical forces, is involved in the emergence and propagation of life? Could not the random coagulation of atoms have fully accounted for the appearance of the first cell? And could not the chance reshuffling of base pairs in DNA have accounted sufficiently for the wide variety of living beings?

I cannot deny that it is initially tempting to pursue this "chance" hypothesis. It seems to have a number of points in its favor. First, there is the argument that given enough time, the improbable becomes increasingly more probable. Physico-chemically speaking, life appears to be a "negentropic," that is, an improbable occurrence. But given a sufficient amount of time an improbable event may eventually occur without violating statistical physical laws. Our earth has existed for approximately five billion years. Within this span of time the thermodynamically improbable event of the living cell with replicative capacities could perhaps accidentally pop up in the cosmic lottery. Even if the *a priori* probabilities of its happening the first time are virtually zero, Jacques Monod holds that it still might happen nonetheless.[1] Furthermore, it has been demonstrated that the amino and nucleic acids which life requires could already have been made plentifully available by rather "impersonal" natural processes. Perhaps their "chance" congealing into DNA and proteins is not so preposterous after all.

A second argument for the "chance" hypothesis is inspired by the serendipitous shapes of many of the biosphere's productions. They may easily cause us to wonder whether anything other than chance is involved in the manipulation of acids that gave them their genetic instructions. The weird creatures in the depths of the oceans, the ichthyosaurs, pterosaurs and other extinct species, the enormous varieties of plants, insects, crustaceans, reptiles, fish and mammals—all of this makes us wonder whether chance might not be as good an "explanation" as any for the morphological richness of life.

Third, the fact that most genetic mutations occur without reference to the welfare of the mutated organism further supports the casualist view and, therefore, challenges the teleologist. Since most mutations are unfavorable and do not aid the organism in its struggle for survival, and since there is so much waste, it is tempting to make chance, aided by natural selection, the controlling factor in evolution.

It is hardly possible, therefore, for us to ignore the view that chance has played a major part in the evolution of species as well as in the origin of life itself. But what is chance? And what exactly is meant by those who say that life appeared by chance and that evolution is a blind process ruled by randomness? Finally, would the fact of chance rule out the religious vision that the cosmos abides within the caring and ultimately meaningful environment of a loving God? To these questions the present chapter will attempt a response.

Chance vs. Design?

Usually discussions of evolution hold out the term "chance" in opposition to "design." Chance is seen as exclusive of design. The evolution of the universe, therefore, is controlled either by chance *or* by design. In this chapter, however, I shall not attempt to refute the chance hypothesis by arguing on behalf of nature's design. Although I would agree that a certain kind of teleology is present in the cosmos, I think the term "design" is too narrow and misleading in any discussion with those who emphasize the role of chance in evolution. Further, I see no reason to hold that purpose in nature excludes a very pronounced element of chance as a prominent factor in evolution. But both "chance" and "design" have connotations that prevent a deeper discussion of the issue of teleology.

The notion of design, for example, typically conjures up images of a "Craftsman" or "Mechanic" who, with complete control and foreknowledge of every detail, methodically plots out the entire panoply of cosmic events and their unfolding through time and space. This image of a Pantocrator (one who actively exercises an omnipotence over all things) is still one of the dominant images of God in the West, though it is questionably justifiable. It resonates with the word "Designer," and so it appears to be logically exclusive of the indeterminacy often implied by the notion of chance.

The "Cosmic Designer" has impressed modernity as a notoriously vague, suffocating and even dehumanizing ideal promulgated by a dying religiosity. And yet the same idea has been defended by traditionalists, appealing to Aristotle, Aquinas and classical theology, as a metaphysical necessity. I suspect that those who defend the hypothesis of chance are often, underneath all the elaborate edifice of rational and scientific argumentation, struggling to escape the oppressive weight of a closed-in world governed by the cosmic Craftsman. And those who persist in reaffirming the design argument are expressing their distaste for a world ruled by chaos. The search for freshness, for breathing room, is, in part at least, the drive behind those who protest the "teleological" view. And the equally significant need for order motivates those who strive to retrieve the classical teleological statements of philosophy and religion. And so the argument, chance vs. design, lumbers along on these two levels.

The best way forward, it seems to me, is to ask whether there is a way of presenting the metaphysical argument for a principle of cosmic order in such a way as simultaneously to satisfy our legitimate requirements for novelty and adventure.

That there is such an alternative I shall propose a bit later. First, however, we should look briefly at some of the confusion surrounding use of the word "chance."

Chance

The word "chance" is used in at least the following five ways:

1. To begin with there is what we might call the *epistemological* usage of the term. According to thinkers as diverse as Laplace, Einstein and Russell, for example, a chance event is one whose cause is unknown. This usage of the term makes chance into a kind of cover-up for our own ignorance. Chance is a blind spot in our understanding rather than an objective fact resident in nature. And since all events must have causes, according to this classical framework, there really are no such things as chance occurrences. "God does not play at dice with the universe," as Einstein put it. Indeterminacy is an illusion.

Strictly speaking, in this view, chance does not exist. It is merely an expression of the limitedness of our knowing. Both theists and atheists are numbered among those who cling to this notion of chance. For some theists chance is actually, in Alexander Pope's words, ". . . direction which thou canst not see." In a hidden way God's omnipotence determines all things. And for the atheist chance is often interpreted as a confused expression cloaking our own ignorance of the iron-clad, impersonal laws of a deterministic universe. In either case chance does not really exist.

2. Another way of understanding "chance" is the *mathematical*. For example, we ask what are the "chances" that a flipped coin will land tails-up. While mathematics cannot decide the answer in any single case, it can formulate laws of probability according to which we can make fairly accurate predictions

regarding the outcome of a large number of coin tossings. In this context "chance" occurrences are *deviations* from statistical regularities. In themselves they are surds, lacking any systematic intelligibility.[2] A common question posed by science today is whether the origin of life and the mutations involved in evolution are such irrational, unplanned and disorderly deviations. It is in this connection especially that the question of purpose in evolution arises. Could life and evolution possibly be the implementation of a divine purposiveness if they are carried along so prominently on a stream of chance happenings?

3. A third context in which the term "chance" is often employed is what I shall call (for lack of a better term) the *existential*. Here "chance" refers to any occurrence which, without interrupting the known laws of natural causation, shows up as an absurdity disturbing the order of our *human* existence. Existential chance appears when two independent physically causal series intersect in such a way as to make us ask fervently: "Why did that have to happen to me or to us?" For example pigeon droppings (representing one causal series) invariably make their way earthward because of the deterministic laws of gravitational attraction. If I on my bicycle, following another independent trajectory, just "chance" to pass underneath such a natural occurrence at the relevant moment, perhaps the fervent uttering will take the form of an oath. The point is that we have here two independent causal series, both blindly following the laws of physics. But the fact that a human being is involved gives their intersection a dimension that would otherwise be absent. One can, of course, think of many much more tragic examples of existential chance. And some modern writers, in fact, interpret our very birth and existence on this planet as such an absurd crossing of incongruous paths.

4. A fourth denotation, this one often given to the term "chance" by scientists, is a *physical* one. A number of modern physicists hold that events at the sub-atomic level are not only

indeterminable or unpredictable by scientific observation, but that they are also unpredictable even in principle. Contrary to the determinists, who see all events as the predictable result of antecedent causes, physical indeterminists insist that at the sub-atomic level there are happenings which are "uncaused," arising spontaneously and unpredictably out of a mysterious depth to which our science of causes cannot penetrate. This speculation of recent physics has encountered a great deal of resistance, even from scientists of the stature of Einstein. Their resistance may be motivated by a fear that nature will slip out of the control of our mechanical and mathematical models for understanding physical reality, or it may be occasioned simply by our innate passion for order and intelligibility. In any case, the hypothesis of physical chance posits an indeterminacy at the base of cosmic reality, and this again forces us to ask whether the natural world is influenced by any sort of ordering principle.

There is an important qualification that needs to be made with respect to this hypothesis of physical chance. Physics can allow for indeterminacy in particular microcosmic occurrences without rejecting the predictability that occurs when large numbers of these occurrences coalesce to make up macroscopic entities. The fact that physical reality is composed of patterned arrangements of more basic constituents enormously softens the effect that minute indeterminacies might have. While God may play at dice with the universe at one level, the plain fact remains that nature exhibits an infinite array of ordered arrangements. Our world, therefore, appears to be a composite of indeterminacy and order.

5. Another intriguing way of using the idea of chance is the *metaphysical*. Here chance is employed as an explanatory concept providing the definitive answer to ultimate questions such as, Why am I here? Why did life appear? Why is there anything at all? Why is there suffering and death, etc.? In this application "Chance" often takes the same place that "God" takes in classical theology. Chance is hypostatized; it is tran-

scendent; it is almighty (though not all-good); it lies beyond the scope of scientific method (since science can deal only with the recurrent, the orderly and the predictable); and finally, Chance comes close to being the object of worship and devotion since it is the metaphysical source of all things. Readers of Jacques Monod's *Chance and Necessity* will find there perhaps the best recent example of the metaphysical enthronement of Chance. James Horigan has noted how for Monod chance functions in a manner parallel to the god-of-the-gaps found in certain caricatures of theism. It is an hypothesis brought onto the scene when human ingenuity and resourcefulness are lacking. It is a deus-ex-machina that puts the lid on further inquiry and delivers us from the need to unravel the story of nature with further careful, patient, rational inquiry.[3]

We can see from this cursory listing that "chance" is as loaded a term as is "design." And I would suggest also that there is an imaginative component associated with employment of the term "chance" that explains its psychological attractiveness to its devotees in the spurious chance vs. design debate. The image of the universe that takes shape in the mental background of those who espouse the chance-hypothesis is often one in which human freedom and creativity are fundamental concerns. It is not entirely surprising that Jacques Monod would attempt to make Sartrean atheistic existentialism with its emphasis on freedom the metaphysical backdrop of *Chance and Necessity*. While it is impossible to reconcile Monod's materialist mechanism with any coherent doctrine of human freedom, his obeisance to the hypostatized idea of Chance displays an underlying concern for a universe in which human freedom would remain a possibility: "The kingdom above or the darkness below . . . it is for us to choose."[4] Even in thinkers not so extreme as Monod there still persists the post-Enlightenment aversion to any metaphysical ultimate that would fix a limit to human growth and potential. The infatuation with chance provides for some an aperture to the requisite breathing-space, whereas the notion of design often seems confining. What we need to do, in response to this legitimate concern for freedom, is to shift the chance vs. design argument to a new plane of discussion, that of order vs. novelty.

Order and Novelty

The chance vs. design debate has long proven to be fruitless. It is a disguise for a more fundamental, perennial controversy, whether the idea of an ultimate principle of order (God) can be reconciled with human freedom and the world's autonomy and indeterminacy. This book is not the place to debate this question, but I think it is important to point it out as an important dimension latent in the deeper layers of the chance vs. design dispute. Moreover, this may be the place at least to outline an alternative that would be sensitive to the underlying issue.

I shall propose that the idea of a transcendent ordering principle is congruous with a universe in which mathematical, physical and existential chance are realities. But such congruity is possible only if this principle of order is at the same time understood as a constant source of novelty as well.[5] For it is in the influx of novelty into our universe that those deviations from order, regularity and tranquillity that we loosely refer to as "chance" occurrences take place. Chance exists because of novelty.

The idea of a "designer" does not lend itself readily to a universe involving chance occurrences. Such an idea too easily leads to the view (the "epistemological" interpretation above) that chance is not a concrete fact of nature, since everything *must* be methodically planned in advance. However, if the world's principle of order is also its source of novelty, then our cosmos of mixed order and chance can be interpreted as logically compatible with such a principle.

The idea of God that I am following in this book includes (but is certainly not exhausted by) the attribute of being both source of order and source of novelty. This idea has been elaborated most expressly by Alfred North Whitehead and his theological followers. I have found their ideas to be faithful not only to important religious intuitions of ultimacy but also to the demands of common human experience, logic and, most importantly for our purposes, modern science. The following is a brief sketch of this Whiteheadian notion of God and how such a notion relates to the fact of chance in nature.

God and Chance: A Whiteheadian Interpretation

That the universe exhibits at least some degree of order, as well as a wide variety of ordered arrangements of physical reality, is obvious. Nobody seriously questions this fact. The issue instead concerns the possible source of what order there is. One hypothesis is to locate the source of order in the human mind. This is the "idealist" position, according to which the mind imposes its patterns onto the inherent formlessness of nature. This "solution," however, merely pushes the problem one step further back: Whence arises the order that is intrinsic to mind (which, as I have emphasized, is also a fact of nature)? We are back at our original question: Why is there any order at all? Why not sheer chaos?

This is where a second position offers itself: order arises *by chance* out of disorder. Given enough time the play of chance, after innumerable attempts at different combinations, becomes locked into regularity, pattern or order. Order arises spontaneously, without purpose, out of the random motion of particles of matter. This is the position of some materialists, for whom "matter" is a kind of ultimate, a quasi-divinity, and chance is the demiurge that shapes the substance of this ultimate into the diverse objects of nature. Our fundamental objections to the materialist position have already been set forth. We should note here in addition, however, that it is inconceivable that the irreducible and ultimate matter of the materialist could itself exist even primordially without already being ordered or patterned in some way or other. Presumably the materialist's almighty matter has an atomic and subatomic make-up, in which case it would already have an enormously complex order. And if one wishes to speculate that there is some other kind of matter beneath the sub-atomic level, the question would still arise in what sense it could be called material or physical without also being ordered in some way or other.

It appears, then, that we are compelled to accept the view that for something even to be actual at all it must possess at least a minimum of order. Total absence of internal patterning would amount to non-actuality. Sheer indeterminateness is nothingness—as ancient mythology, Hegel and Sartre (not to mention Whitehead) have all recognized. To be actual is to be something definite, and this implies being ordered.[6]

So our question still remains: Why any order at all? Why not no-thing? Why not utter indeterminateness? Surely it is not incoherent for us to hypothesize a third alternative to the idealist and the materialist ones. This third position postulates an ultimate principle of order from which emanates the forms of order into which the occasions of experience making up the physical universe are patterned. This principle of order need not be conceived of as *imposing* order on nature. Rather it may be thought of as a source of *possible* patterings relevant to the cosmos at each phase of its becoming. Instead of coercing the universe into prefabricated molds it lures or persuades the cosmos toward the actualization of new possibilities.[7] Thus the term "Designer" seems inappropriate as the primary image of this metaphysical principle.

The universe is always capable of deviating from the patterns offered by our postulated ordering principle. If it were not capable of putting up a resistance to the proposal of new modes of order, it would not then be a world. Instead it would dissolve into the ordering principle itself. Without some element of recalcitrance the cosmos would be nothing more than an emanation of the ordering principle and have no intrinsic being or autonomy of its own. Indeterminacy of some sort and degree must therefore be an aspect of any universe which is not a mere emanation of its ultimate source of order. This means that the universe is not governed by any rigid teleological scheme. There is room in it for those occurrences that we confusedly refer to as chance. And yet there is the possibility that forms of order may gradually be teased out of the chaos of indeterminacy.

It is in the nature of our hypothesized principle of order that it is non-interfering and unobtrusive. It is Tao-like in its functioning, and yet, as we have seen, it is causal in the deepest sense of the term, not in a mechanical but in a "formal" way. Because of its unobtrusive, formatively causal, rather than mechanically coercive, mode of influencing the universe it is inevitable that there would be deviations from the intelligibility inherent in order. These deviations are what we call chance occurrences. They are real and not just our own epistemological blind-spots. But this is not the whole story. For even these deviations, while unintelligible from the point of view of one frame of order, might not be without intelligibility from within a wider angle of vision. There are dangers in our phrasing here which we shall clarify later on, but it is legitimate to state that at least some things which appear without intelligibility from an earlier perspective may in principle become intelligible within a later and wider perspective.[8] If this is the case, then, it may be simply impossible for us ever to have a controlling and objectively comprehensive understanding of what chance really is.

And yet this is not to deny that chance is in some sense real, rather than an epistemological evasion. For the principle of order to which we have alluded is also understood here as the ultimate source of novelty. And whenever novelty invades a situation of order the result is at least momentary deviation from the fixed arrangements of the past. A certain degree of chaos will accompany the emergence of a more complex order. As the past gives way to further intensification of order, the momentary breakdown of harmonious patterning may give rise to occurrences for which the word "chance" is appropriate. When God is understood as principle not only of order but also of novelty, the idea of God is compatible with the fact of chance.[9]

Chance and Nature's Hierarchy

The occurrence of chance is also an inevitable facet of a hierarchical universe. When one level of nature's hierarchy (say the level of life or mind) harnesses a lower level (that of matter) it is not surprising that the lower level will not be in every respect congenial to the imposition of the novel organizational principles of the higher. As the higher level imposes boundary conditions on the lower processes, the latter may continue blindly and independently of the comprehensive net flung by the former. There would be no such thing as chance if the universe were not hierarchically structured. If the universe were merely a one-dimensional causal series of physical occurrences, it is difficult to imagine how "chance" would ever show up. The very fact of our noticing and being bothered about chance occurrences is a clue to the fact of a hierarchical universe in which causal paths involving distinct levels at times cross each other to our dismay or delight. As I pointed out earlier, there is an "existential" undertone in all of our discussions of chance. And this is because we also, as conscious and purposive beings, are part of this hierarchical universe where many levels are constantly intersecting one another.

It is the hierarchical structure of nature that makes it unnecessary for us to imagine that the cosmos is simply a roulette wheel out of which a living cell with replicative capacities accidentally turned up all of a sudden one day long ago. Such an occurrence required the careful, painstaking preparation of an appropriate context. In evolution distinct levels have emerged, each one of them eventually falling into stable, repetitive and predictable routines. And like notches of a ratchet the existence of these stable levels (the sub-atomic, atomic, molecular, biotic, psychological) prevents the wheel of nature from going back to point zero with each turn. It is quite possible that the emergence of the first living cell involved an aspect of randomness. It had to be, by definition, a unique event, an unprecedented occurrence. But the context in which life made its sudden appearance should not be imagined as a kind of chaotic soup of chemicals. Speaking more realistically, the envi-

ronment into which the biosphere flooded was already a hierarchical assembly of subassemblies, each level of which was
endowed with an order and irreversibility that prevented the
whole edifice from constantly sinking back into complete chaos.[10] In such a hierarchical framework the initial appearance of
a new and higher level always has to be a unique event. But we
should not confuse its uniqueness with utter randomness (as
Jacques Monod has done). If, as I am maintaining, nature is an
emergent hierarchy of levels, the initial appearance of each
successive new level is going to appear baffling from the point
of view of our understanding of the preceding ones. To explain
its coming into being only as a result of pure chance, however,
is to betray an inability to think hierarchically about nature.
The issue of chance and purpose brings us, therefore, to the
question of the plausibility of hierarchical thinking. I shall take
this question up in the following chapter.

Conclusion

Chance is not incompatible with order. And when "order"
involves an emergent hierarchy of levels in which a trend
toward novelty is prominent, we must be prepared to admit the
fact of chance into our cosmic picture. It is easy enough to do so
when we are speaking of the epistemological, physical and
mathematical dimensions of chance. The troublesome questions
concern the existential and metaphysical usages of the term.
Expecially when causal series intersect so as to cause us pain
do we wonder whether our universe is ruled ultimately by
chance. At this point our discussion of chance converges with
what is called the theodicy problem, and this will be the subject
of Chapters 9 and 10.

7.

Purpose and Nature's Hierarchy

The objective of this and the following chapter is to set forth two schemes according to which the cosmos may be viewed as teleological. Again, in keeping with the methodological modesty of previous chapters, no pretense will be made that we can demonstrate the existence of purpose in nature. The most we can do is to argue for the plausibility of some kind of universal purpose in the cosmos as we understand it in the light of modern science. Though we cannot demonstrate the existence of purpose in nature, we may at least explain why it eludes our attempts at demonstration. Precisely because of its transcendent Tao-like nature any hypothetical teleological principle would lie beyond the grasp of our controlling modes of inquiry. Our sense of its presence would have to be mediated through a non-controlling mode of cognition the nature of which will be set forth in the present chapter.

The first of our two schemes is framed in terms of the hierarchical structure of nature and the second in terms of aesthetic experience. The first is proposed on the basis of Polanyi's thought, the second on Whitehead's. While the two schemes are compatible with one another, they each approach the issue of cosmic meaning by way of different aspects of cosmic structure. Therefore I shall treat each interpretation separately.

The Emergent View of Nature

The cosmologies implied in mythic, religious and most philosophical systems of the past have been hierarchical in nature.[1] They have usually delineated four realms of cosmic being: mineral, plant, animal, man. And above or encompassing these they have intuited another level, that of "ultimate reality," variously named and imaged in different traditions. Our ordinary language and thought are still conditioned by hierarchical thinking. And even evolutionary theory continues to rely upon the hierarchical distinctions of levels, though it envisages them as stages in a horizontally linear movement with the lines of demarcation somewhat blurred. I have argued in Chapter 4 that the obvious physical and historical continuity tying the "higher" phases of evolution to the lower does not at all rule out the possibility of an ontological discontinuity. In other words the essence of hierarchical thinking still remains valid even in an evolutionary world-view. I am not entirely happy with the expression "hierarchy of levels," since it fails to accentuate sufficiently the processive nature of reality. It is a notion that seems to fit more readily the Hellenistic than the evolutionary view of the cosmos. And yet I cannot entirely dispense with it. Hierarchical thinking of some sort is necessary if our evolutionary universe is more than one-dimensional. If it is not reducible to the level of matter, then such a universe can be conceptualized only as a variety of levels, dimensions or fields ordered hierarchically. The problem, though, is how to fit the hierarchical onto the evolutionary model.

The key notion in such an alliance is that of "emergence."[2] An emergent universe is an evolutionary one in which each successive phase adds something qualitatively new. The emergent phase is more than the sum of its antecedents. In contrast to the notion of emergence is that of "resultance."[3] A resultant universe would be one in which each successive evolutionary development is nothing more than the additive "result" of antecedent component physical parts and movements. Such is the universe of materialism. In an emergent universe the influence of extraneous formative causation is the ingredient required to channel the mass-energy continuum into novel and ontologically distinct levels of being. In Chapter 5 I attempted to show why we may postulate the presence of formative causation in nature even though it is not detectable as part of the mass-energy continuum accessible to science. I would now like to direct my discussion more focally toward the question of why any conceivable *final* causation in an emergent universe would also evade our demands for evidence. How would purpose insinuate itself into a dynamically hierarchical universe without being overwhelmingly noticeable?

Purpose in an Emergent Universe

In any hierarchical structure the higher levels embrace or "comprehend" the lower, but the lower are unable to comprehend the higher. This is what may be called the "hierarchical principle." We have already seen an instance of this principle at work in our speculation on the relationship of life to matter. I have followed Polanyi's contention that there are organizational principles operative in the universe which formatively influence the specific sequences of nucleic acids in DNA, and with Sheldrake I have postulated the existence of morphogenetic fields which canalize the processes of growth and development in organisms. These formative causes and fields sound like sheer imaginings unless we view them in accordance with the requirements of the hierarchical principle. According to this principle the elusiveness to science of organizational biotic principles and morphogenetic fields is to be expected. These principles and fields are not on the same level as the molecular and, therefore, cannot be grasped with the same degree of verificational control. From the vantage point of an analysis of lower levels the higher cannot be comprehended. The demand by materialists that these principles and fields manifest themselves tangibly is at root a repudiation of the hierarchical principle. Thus the issue of science and religion revolves very closely around the question of the legitimacy of hierarchical thinking.

If there is any sort of final causation influencing our

universe, we may safely conjecture that it would reside fundamentally at a higher, more comprehensive level than any accessible to our mind's grasp. And we need not hold that the
presence of such a teleological dimension would interfere with,
violate, twist, or modify the "laws" of physics, chemistry, biology, psychology, etc., that define each successive level. By definition, in other words, universal purpose would not stand as one
"fact" among others evident to our observation. Biological
materialists expect that if there really is a teleological aspect to
the cosmos it would be obvious as one among other "facts" of
biology. Ernst Mayr, for example, writes:

> The proponents of teleological theories, for all their efforts,
> have been unable to find any mechanisms (except supernatu-
> ral ones) that can account for their postulated finalism. The
> possibility that any such mechanism can exist has now been
> virtually ruled out by the findings of molecular biology.[4]

By its implicit demand that teleology display itself on the level
of molecular mechanisms, this Harvard biologist's statement
exhibits the difficulty many scientists have today with hierarchical thinking. Unless a reality is part of the molecular spectrum its existence is deemed suspect.

I have very little hope of converting thinkers like Mayr to
the hierarchical vision. E.F. Schumacher is correct when he
says that it is their particular "faith" perspective that leads
them to place all reality at the level of the molecular. It is their
"faith" that dictates to them that all reality can be collapsed
into "matter" and understood exhaustively in terms of that
level.[5] The most that I can do, therefore, is to show why it is
that any conceivable higher level cannot be grasped in terms of
the lower.

The Unobtrusiveness of Higher Levels

The higher levels do not interrupt or interfere with the
lower. That is why they cannot appear or be understood at the
level of the lower. The higher, in Polanyi's terms, "dwell in"

and "rely upon" but are not reducible to the lower and do not suspend the workings of the lower.[6] We have seen, for example, that biotic processes do not interrupt or violate the chemical laws that bond carbon to hydrogen, oxygen and nitrogen. Life's organizational principles and morphogenetic fields do not require that physical laws be suspended in order for life to make its entrance into the scheme of things. Such vitalism is not essential. There is no need to hold that the laws of physics are reversed in the evolutionary process. Instead the very existence of life depends upon the reliable and predictable workings of invariant physico-chemical laws. If carbon "decided" occasionally and capriciously to modify its specific bonding properties we would not have the dependable physical infrastructure necessary for life. Or, moving up to a higher level, if the chemistry of the brain were altered, then the capacity of mental principles to function would be affected also. Life and mind both rely upon and dwell in the lower levels, and they require the reliable performance of chemical and physical laws as a condition for their actualization. The town planner does not alter the specific techniques of bricklaying in order to construct a town; rather he makes use of these already proven techniques, imposes organizational patterns upon them, but in no way interrupts them. Similarly, the organizational principles operative in a hierarchical universe at the levels of life and mind do not interrupt, but make use of, the laws of physics and chemistry.

This is what I mean by the unobtrusiveness of higher levels. They operate in a *globally* organizational fashion and, therefore, cannot be specified by an analysis of the subordinate particulars of any system. An analysis of the brickwork in a town, no matter how meticulously executed, will not yield an understanding of what a town is. The town's overall design cannot be found in the joints and component parts of the brickwork. The global organizational pattern does not appear as one fact among others at the level of the town's masonry. It does not obtrude; it cannot insert itself into this lower level. It can comprehend or globally encompass the level of brickwork, but it cannot be comprehended by an analysis of that level.[7]

We cannot *a priori* rule out the possibility that the principles of life and mind relate to the level of matter in an analogously unobtrusive fashion. Perhaps there are extraneous organizational principles somehow influencing (not in any rigid manner, however) lower systems so that the latter take on a specific shape corresponding to the influence of the higher level or field. While we cannot reject the possibility of such fields of influence, neither of course can we render them visible. By definition they do not intrude. Their influence is one of effective non-interference. They comprehend without being comprehensible. They are not subject to our controlling knowledge. They operate according to the mode of Taoism's *wu-wei*. Like the Tao they accomplish much without making themselves obvious.

Cosmic Purpose

If there is a divine scheme of purposefulness enveloping and grounding the multiple levels and fields of influence in an emergent universe, then we should not expect or demand that its presence be obvious to us either. If there is a teleological dimension that transcends our own lives and minds, the hierarchical principle should remain our guide when we ask for evidence of its reality. This principle insists that the higher comprehends the lower and dwells in it but is not capable of being grasped in a controlling way by the lower. Each level can only order what lies beneath it. It leaves itself open to being ordered by the levels above it, but is not able to control the higher. If there is any purpose in the universe, therefore, we would not be able to arrive at a controlling knowledge of it. Hierarchical thinking is quite comfortable with this confession.

The Epistemology of Control

We must ask, though, why hierarchical thinking has been rejected to such a large extent by modernity. In a sense the answer to this question will respond to our own inquiry as to why teleological thinking seems so implausible today.

I am convinced that Huston Smith has accurately diagnosed the source of modern anti-hierarchical ideology when he traces it to what he calls (following Ernest Gellner) "the epistemology of control." Although I am not entirely happy with Smith's recent books on science and religion, especially since they fail adequately to appropriate evolutionary thought, I think there is value in his own hierarchical vision and his critique of the epistemology of control.[8]

The epistemology of control has its roots not only in our Western philosophical tradition, but also in the very nature of human beings. It is essentially our obsession with power that leads us to think that whatever is real must somehow be subject in principle to mastery by our own intellects. The epistemology of control is simply the carry-over of the will to power into the realm of the mind. It is a refusal to acknowledge the possibility that there are fields of reality that lie off limits, even in principle, to the control of rational consciousness. To open ourselves to such a possibility would require a renunciation of our impulse to control. And this is too high a price for many of us to pay.[9]

Since the Enlightenment, when the West began to experience the full emergence of the rational subject, we have become increasingly dizzy with the apparent capacity of our subjectivity to master its world. The mind's sense of liberation from its perennial cosmic matrix has led it to turn back with vengefulness upon the parent that kept it in bondage for so long. This revenge is manifested not only in the destructiveness of modern technological cultures toward the natural world, but also in a relentless epistemological refusal of the mind to surrender itself to anything larger than itself. Rather than acknowledge that it is itself comprehended and contextualized by a transcending field of influence, the mind would prefer to remain in its position of pretended mastery, even if this leads to the isolation of despair.

Of course, this drift of subjectivity away from the cosmos, an alienation prepared for by ancient dualistic mythology, cannot be mended by a restoration of pre-rational, naive conscious-ness. In the history of consciousness there is no "going home again" to an undifferentiated paradise of uncritical belonging to nature. Once and for all our consciousness has differentiated itself from its cosmic womb. And dualistic mythology has been the midwife of this parturition. In Paul Ricoeur's terminology, we cannot return to a pre-critical naiveté.[10] Neither, however, can we abide forever the estrangement of our minds from nature. Can we not find some sort of reconciliation of mind with nature in a "post-critical naiveté"? Cannot the mind once again feel at home in the cosmos without repressing its critically rational capacities? Need the differentiation of mind from na-ture entail a separation of the two as it has for most modern thought?

In order to bring about a post-critical reconciliation of mind and nature we need a wider and deeper sense of the cosmos than our religious ancestors had or than modern science has given us since the seventeenth century. I doubt very much if we have yet achieved, let alone surrendered, to such a wider cos-mology. Correspondingly, we would need a wider teleology than that of the Greek philosophers or theistic religions of the past if we are once again to see purpose in the scheme of things. Our sense of the cosmic hierarchy today cannot be the same as that of our ancestors. It must be broadened, deepened and framed in terms of the notion of dynamic "fields" of influence and evolutionary theory.

Evolutionary theory, geology, astronomy, biology and modern physics are giving us a new sense of the infinite depths of the cosmos today. They are also calling us to a new form of surrender to mystery, of renunciation of our adolescent aspira-tions to control. A new sense of being encompassed by the unfathomable has taken hold of those who have deeply felt our post-Newtonian world. Scientists of the stature of Einstein, though they reject traditional ideas of God, have called for a religious response of wonder and awe in the face of the cosmic mysteries. And yet, to a great extent scientific thinkers have clung to the ideal that the objective of science is to eliminate mystery.[11] A Promethean refusal to surrender still dominates academic and popular presentations of scientific discoveries. The epistemology of control still reigns. The consequence of this attitude is that it rules out in principle any possibility of there being a more comprehensive dimension transcending the level of our own minds. As Smith says, "To expect a transcendental object to appear on a viewing screen wired by an epistemology that is set for control would be tantamount to expecting color to appear on a television screen that was built for black and white."[12]

Faith

There is an alternative mode of cognition that instead of being dominated by the impulse to control is a product of a desire to surrender to the possible mysteriousness of reality. The name we may give to this type of consciousness is faith. Faith as surrender to mystery has little meaning outside of the context of a hierarchical universe. But in an emergent, hierarchical universe faith is the kind of knowing whereby we at the human level of evolution leave ourselves open to being grasped by a more encompassing field of influence.[13] In the cosmic hierarchy the lower cannot comprehend the higher. But the lower can *leave itself open* to being harnessed and organized by a higher principle.[14] Physico-chemical processes leave themselves open to being ordered by biotic principles. Life processes leave themselves open to being ordered by mental or human processes. Faith, in the context of an emergent universe, is simply the stance that we at the human level of emergence would take when we surrender ourselves to being influenced by whatever higher field there may be encompassing the cosmic hierarchy. The fact that this higher field of influence does not show up on our screens wired by the impulse to control is insufficient warrant for us to banish the possibility of its reality. If there is a teleological aspect to our universe its presence would not be detectable by the controlling techniques of scientific method. Instead it would only make itself known to minds which have opened themselves to being ordered or influenced by the higher dimension. This opening of ourselves toward the incomprehensible is what I mean by faith.

I realize that I have enormously oversimplified the notion of faith here. Much more is involved, and different contexts would require our accentuating other aspects of faith. My main concern here, though, is simply to situate faith in the context of an emergent universe, to understand faith cosmologically rather than psychologically. And in such a context I would understand it not as a dogmatic posture but as an exploratory dimension of the emergent cosmos itself. Through faith the evolutionary universe at the hominized level reaches out for and opens itself up to a more comprehensive dimension. What the final result of this self-surrender will be we have no definitive way of knowing. We can only imagine it symbolically. Religious symbols and myths throughout the ages have been one, but only one, way in which our consciousness has allowed the transcendent to take root in, to dwell in and rely upon, our human level of emergence. I understand faith as a much broader term than religion, though. And I think faith is present in movements and individuals that are not "religious" in any conventional sense of the term. Wherever there is an exploratory openness to the new, together with a humble abandonment of the will to subject the universe to the contours of our own limited intellects, there is faith. There is an element of the Pascalian wager, the Kierkegaardian leap, the existentialist risk, involved in any renunciation of the epistemology of control. There is the Abrahamic willingness to set forth into lands unknown, a surrender to the possibility that our lives and minds may be given a meaning by something infinitely larger than themselves. To accept the possibility of a purposeful universe is not as easy as its critics suggest. In fact the surrender of faith is a painful one. It requires our leaving behind the familiar contours of the world we think we have objectively mastered. It demands that we commit ourselves to the adventure of exploratory hope. Such a commitment has never been easy.

8.

Beauty

In the previous chapter I suggested that the possibility of purpose in the universe may be understood in terms of a hierarchical conception of the cosmos. It was especially Michael Polanyi's thought that provided the central ideas I developed there. In this chapter I shall fall back upon aspects of Whitehead's philosophy once again in order to provide yet another way of thinking of our universe in teleological terms. In both instances the kind of teleology being proposed is what must be called a "loose" teleology. I use this expression, another which I have taken over from Polanyi, in order to distance my approach from the restrictive opinion that the universe has built into it some rigidly pre-determined destiny.[1]

Let me state what I mean by a loose teleology in rather simple terms. If our universe were to start all over again with the Big Bang there is no need to hold that it would have unfolded in its evolution in a manner anything like the present one. The role of chance and indeterminacy, the specific choices of the natural selection process, and even possible alternative sets of physical laws would have caused a quite different world to evolve. Or if we were to turn back the evolutionary clock two billion years and reconstruct the "primordial soups" from which the molecules of life were fashioned, we would have no guarantee that eventually there would have been fish, reptiles, birds, monkeys, or ... humans. There is no necessity that evolution take one and only one course.[2] What does seem quite possible, though, is that the cosmos would still have embarked upon a course of complexification. There still might have been a straining toward the further realization of more intensely complex arrangements of physical reality. In other words our universe would still have been an adventure of evolution. But there is no a priori necessity that the cosmos have developed in one particular fashion. That it aim toward more intense forms of ordered novelty may be a metaphysical necessity, even if the actualization of this aim is often frustrated. But it is not essential for cosmic teleology that the universe have arrived at precisely this present state of evolution.

I think the best way of understanding cosmic purpose in our loose sense is to propose that it consists essentially in the aim toward beauty.[3] Perhaps from the limitedness of our own perspective we can say no more, but at least we can say this much. An aesthetic notion of cosmic purpose is capable of embracing the mythic and religious representations of human aspiration as well as accommodating the modern scientific understanding of the universe. An aesthetic rendition of cosmic teleology allows us to speak of a pervasive cosmic aim without having to be too restrictive in specifying the exact goal toward which cosmic process may be oriented.

Within this very broad scheme centering on the notion of beauty it is still possible to entertain more specific proposals as to the ultimate meaning of things. For example, a number of teleological theories attempt to understand the cosmic process as one that aims toward the enhancement of consciousness.[4] I have no objection to this teleological perspective. And there is increasing evidence from the sciences that our universe has evolved from rudimentary toward more intensely conscious structures. However, I shall attempt to show that an aesthetic reading of cosmic purpose is more comprehensive than consciousness-oriented teleologies (such as that of Teilhard de Chardin). It is more comprehensive since it takes into account more caringly those segments of cosmic process that appear to us to be regressive, to move away from further enhancement of consciousness and away from the ideals we set up for our human existence. The universe is not in every way directional in the manner we would perhaps like it to be. Thus if we are to speak of cosmic purpose in a plausible way we must remain fully cognizant of the meandering and confusing nature of its evolutionary trajectory. I think an aesthetic perspective is comprehensive enough to accommodate and salvage all the waywardness of this evolutionary complexity.

The purpose of the cosmos, then, is its aim toward beauty. How would such an aim render the cosmic process purposeful? In response to this question we must point out first of all that beauty is a value.[5] And it is the struggle to realize value that makes any process purposeful. Thus if the cosmic process is dominated by an urge toward realization of beauty, it may be called purposeful. The question though is whether and how we can understand value in aesthetic terms. We are so conditioned to think of value in moral or ethical terms that we may be bewildered by any attempt to express ultimate value in terms of criteria of beauty.[6]

When critics of teleology reject the idea of purpose in the universe their suspicions are almost always framed according to ethical criteria. For these critics the universe is condemned for not corresponding in its behavior to that of the ethical person: therefore, it is not good. If it is not ordered toward the ethical good, then it is not purposeful. In its evolution it displays a marked disregard for life, allowing all living beings and species eventually to pass into oblivion; and in its relentless laws of inertia and natural selection it exhibits crude indifference toward the dignity of persons. Nature seems to operate more by caprice, indifference or malice than by concern for its children. Its cruel experimenting with various forms of life in order eventually to discard them certainly makes it less than an adequate model for our own conduct. This is why Bertrand Russell says that the universe is unworthy of us. Our own goodness far outshines that of the universe in which we live. How can such a universe be purposeful?[7]

If we were to evaluate the universe purely in terms of ethical criteria of value we might be tempted toward cosmic pessimism. Even according to such ethical criteria, however, I think in all fairness we have to acknowledge the extent to which the universe also manifests what we may call "care." For the most part the universe sustains us instead of crushing us. Although the evidence is not unambiguous there is an aura of sustenance throughout nature. There are catastrophes of course, resulting from the varying degrees of hierachical independence of one level from another. But more remarkable than these episodes of chaos is the overall environing affirmation given to species and individuals. We cannot overlook this fact nor fail in gratitude toward it.[8]

Even after making this qualification, however, I think that it is a mistake to argue for cosmic purpose on the grounds that the cosmos conforms to our ethical ideal of care. For the fact is that this care is not all-pervasive. There are no guarantees for our safety. There is tragedy, suffering and death. There are logical and ethical contradictions in our worldly experience. There are the absurd oppositions existing between life and death, growth and decay, pleasure and pain, ecstasy and sorrow, light and darkness, good and evil, order and chaos. It would be naive to build a cosmological perspective without acknowledging these tragic conflicts.

The problem with the ethical perspective is that it cannot deal with these contradictions as such. It measures everything in terms of moral order and remains baffled by the chaotic. On the other hand an aesthetic perspective is quite at home in the realm of contradictions, for its very nature allows it to transform them into a harmony of contrasts. And I shall propose that the caring aspect of the cosmic process can be better expressed in aesthetic than in ethical terms. Although, no doubt, an aesthetic understanding of cosmic order is less than adequate also, I think that it is superior to and broader than the ethical model as an approach to understanding what may be meant by cosmic order or purpose.

Aesthetic Value

When we use the term "aesthetic" we are talking about beauty. Is it possible to put into words why things strike us as beautiful and why some things strike as more beautiful than others? Whitehead's thought provides the concepts for just such a clarification.[9] First of all, beauty entails a synthesis of contrasts. Without contrasting elements there is sheer monotony, and monotony is not beautiful. At the same time beauty implies a resolution of contradiction or conflict, that is, it requires a harmoniousness or order that overrules chaos. When elements in a painting, poem or musical composition clash so as to destroy overall harmoniousness then the aesthetic quality of the work of art is diminished or lost. Therefore, we call beautiful any expression, entity or experience that transforms or resolves contradictions into contrasts. In order for such a resolution to take place, however, the conflicting elements must be situated within a framework of harmony that transcends and, therefore, softens the local clash of contradictory aspects. Within such a wider framework the localized disharmony can become a nuance that enriches the whole instead of a clash that destroys it.

Beauty, we have said, requires a harmony of contrasts. But at times the harmony may tend to overrule the contrast and melt it down to homogeneity. When this occurs beauty has given way to monotony. The beautiful is threatened on two sides, by chaos on one side and monotony or triviality on the other. Beauty is a balancing act between the extremes of chaos and banality. It is precarious, and therefore is precious. Beauty is a synthesis of harmony and complexity, order and novelty, stability and motion, form and dynamics.

Beauty is a harmony of contrasts. Let me illustrate this point beginning with a very simple example. When I simultaneously strike two adjacent keys on a piano the half-note interval between them causes a rather disharmonious, even unpleasant and unsatisfying sound to emerge. The sound amounts more to "noise" than to harmony, and so I would refrain from calling it beautiful. However, if in the course of playing a musical composition I strike the same two keys again simultaneously, then their local dissonance may actually contribute to the overall aesthetic intensity of the whole piece. The orderly patterning of sounds that makes up the whole musical composition resolves the local contradiction (dissonance) into an aesthetically satisfying contrast. This resolution of contradiction into contrast is of the essence of beauty.

A second example may be taken from the art of painting. If I were to isolate a small segment of a great painting (say a few square inches) and prescind momentarily from the whole canvas, I would find in the fragment shades of color, texture and theme that added up to chaos or to monotony. In its isolation I would not find the fragment aesthetically satisfying. But when I resituate this isolated segment back onto the whole painting I find that its formerly chaotic or monotonous qualities are resolved by the overall harmony and nuance into factors that contribute to the aesthetic value of the whole. A wider perspective can transform locally unaesthetic elements into aesthetic ones. There is no reason for us to reject the possibility that in a similar way the chaotic and monotonous episodes of all experience, ours as well as nature's in general, may also contribute to the value of the whole when viewed from a cosmic perspective (to which of course we do not ourselves have access).

A third example may be derived from literature. In reading a novel I may find that several episodes are independently developed early in the novel in such a way that they seem to have nothing to do with each other. Taken in themselves these fragments may appear either boring or unintelligible. I may find it a torture to go through them and may even be tempted to overlook them altogether. Yet by the time I reach the end of the novel I am glad I took the time to explore them. For in the final analysis the episodes which in themselves seemed monotonous or unintelligibly complex now enhance my appreciation of the novel as a whole. They have a significance and a connectedness when viewed from a wider perspective that they do not appear to have when I am too close to them.

Now from the Whiteheadian point of view the cosmos is such an aesthetic reality. Both in its constituent occasions and in its overall reality the universe is a process of synthesizing and unifying its composite aspects into novel moments of present aesthetic "enjoyment." As each occasion feels its past it "orders" the diversity entering into it from the past into a novel feeling of aesthetic harmony and contrast. And as the creative advance of the universe brings more and more novelty into the picture, the events of the past are continually given a new and unanticipated significance. As the sea of events that make up the cosmos broadens and deepens, the meaning of each individual happening is itself intensified and widened. Its final meaning, therefore, cannot be determined from its own limited perspective any more than we can determine the meaning of the early episodes of a novel without reading it to the end.

The purpose of the universe, therefore, cannot be adequately stated from within our own situatedness. We are ourselves part of the canvas. We are characters in the story. We do not have the perspective whereby to give a final assessment of our own significance, or that of any phase of evolution, in the total scheme of things. We may in part understand the idea of God, however, as the cosmic artist or story-teller by whom the significance of every event and every life is guaranteed, though we cannot articulate exactly in what this significance consists.

Thus an aesthetic understanding of the universe is able to express the religious sense that all things are "cared for" in an ultimate though hidden way. And it can do so more plausibly than can any ethical vision of things. The ethical vision is governed by the concern that justice be done, if possible here and now.[10] And, of course, such concern is absolutely essential in the maintenance of civilization and the quality of life. Yet, as most great religious visionaries have themselves taught, the ethical vision is not ultimate. It must be transcended. Our ethical standards are not the final judge of the significance of things, neither of human lives nor of history, nor of the universe. In placing the cosmos in an aesthetic perspective we are following the impulse of a religious vision which acknowledges the inadequacy of our ethical criteria of good and evil. We must revision "good" and "evil" in an aesthetic manner and evaluate the universe according to a deeper understanding of these usually ethically biased terms.

From an aesthetic perspective the goodness or value of an

entity or event is measured by the degree to which contrasting elements are harmonized. The intensity of anything's value is determined by the extent to which its polar components are unified in an orderly pattern. Aesthetically understood, value entails a synthesis of complexity with order, novelty with continuity, nuance with harmony, richness with stability. An aesthetic pattern transforms these apparent contradictions into pleasing contrasts. And we spontaneously tend to value things that combine these contrasts more than we do things that are homogeneous and monotonous in their make-up. We appreciate the human brain more than we do a lump of clay because the brain integrates into an intense unity an incredible complexity, nuance, richness and novelty. Similarly we value art, literature and music in proportion to the intensity of their balancing nuance into satisfying contrasts. Somehow we sense that the complexity of a great work of art could easily have gotten out of control and undermined any efforts toward harmonizing its many facets into an intense unity. And so we inwardly applaud the precious achievement of balance and order when there are so many ingredients that could have led to imbalance and disorder. The more intense the aesthetic achievement, the more we value it.

The hero or genius arouses our admiration for essentially the same reasons as a work of art. Heroism, for example, is beautiful because it is the result of integrating a multiplicity of contrasting experiences (strength and frustration, joy and tragedy, rebellion and resignation, life and death) into the unity of a single person's story. Genius is beautiful because it requires the integration into a creative unity of a multiplicity of ideas, feelings and experiences that could lead to madness in a narrower personality. Because of the precarious nature of heroism and genius we esteem them more than the everyday modes of human existence. Similarly we might value a universe in which contradictions are constantly being unified into an aesthetic whole: entropy and evolution; order and chaos; novelty and continuity; permanence and perishing. In the following chapter I shall return to this theme of perishing.

Conclusion

The beauty toward which the universe strives is enough to imbue it with purpose. Yet from the limited vantage point that I occupy in this evolving world it often seems that discord is more prominent than harmony. Much of my immediate environment is unintelligible. And as I extend my imagination and questioning beyond my situation outward toward the universe I become even more bewildered by what it is all about. I may be tempted to take my own confusion and project it onto the universe. I may read my own intellectual, moral, and especially aesthetic insensitivity into the cosmos as a whole. I may see the cosmos as lacking purpose.

However, the aesthetic model of cosmic purpose suggests that my own experience may be lacking in perspective. Perhaps there is a vantage point on the universe that I do not have, given the confines of my own extremely limited situation. I cannot exclude the possibility that my own experience is only an infinitesimal segment of a universal canvas, only a fragmentary movement in a cosmic composition, a brief episode in nature's narrative. For perhaps there is a wider angle of vision on the universe to which I do not myself have access. Perhaps this wider perspective, lying hierarchically above my own level of comprehension, is able to unify into an aesthetic whole those contradictions, monotonies and absurdities that I deem most insurmountable. Perhaps from this perspective my life has a significance, a purpose, a meaning which I cannot grasp hold of in a controlling manner. Perhaps, though, if I risk the surrender to such a possibility I may feel, even here and now, a portion of the peace that comes with the resolution of contradictions into contrasts. I may feel perhaps only briefly and episodically the beauty toward which the universe tends, the beauty of which I am only a small but significant part.

9.

Permanence and Perishing

I suggested in the previous chapter that an aesthetic perspective on the cosmos is better able to support the religious view that all is ultimately cared for than are the usually employed ethical criteria for evaluating things. From our finite standpoint we are tempted to demand that the universe conform to our "high" standards of moral order. And when we find that neither we nor the other species in evolution are treated according to these standards we are inclined to indict the universe for its moral indifference. Thence we may be inclined to reject any intrinsic cosmic meaning and set up ourselves as superior to this uncaring world.

Such an indictment, I am arguing, comes prematurely (though understandably and forgivably). It is a judgment made on the basis of our limited moralistic apprehension of order with the implicit demand that the totality of cosmic reality conform to this particular order. A classic instance of the demand that the universe adjust itself to our human calculation of order may be found in Dostoevski's novel, *The Brothers Karamazov*. There Ivan rejects this universe since it does not fit the contours of his "Euclidean" reason, which Ivan takes to be the final measure of things. The simple fact that innocent children suffer, and therefore that the ethical value of justice is violated, is enough to prove the overall incongruity and absurdity of this universe. Hence Ivan would respectfully return his entrance ticket to this world rather than embrace it with its injustice.

In this and the following chapter I would like to expand on our aesthetic notion of cosmic purpose, keeping Ivan's protest in mind. I shall be dealing, in other words, with the problem of evil, the so-called question of theodicy. Ultimately any discussion of cosmic purpose leads us into this problem. In the present chapter I shall ask whether it is possible to conceive of the universe as a context of care in spite of the most basic instance of evil, the fact that things perish. And in the following chapter I shall dig deeper into the notion of evil by relating it to the fact that our universe is not only a process in which everything perishes but a process in which novelty is continually entering onto the cosmic scene, causing the breakdown of previous orderly arrangements and bringing about suffering.

The most blatant evidence of the existence of evil is the plain and simple fact that things perish.[1] Perishing means the loss of order, the collapse into disorder and indefiniteness. And where there is indefiniteness, there is nothingness. Perishing means loss, loss of actuality and value. Therefore, perishing is evil. Unless there is permanence, then, there can be no order or value. So if the universe is purposeful there would somehow have to be a solution to the fact of perishing. Something would have to save the stream of events from utter annihilation.

Adding poignancy to the fact that things perish is the fact that the most beautiful things are the most perishable of all. The more beautiful something is the more precarious it is. Genuine beauty entails such a fragile balance between the extremes of complexity and harmony that the slide into either confusion or triviality is more of a possibility than with those things or events that are closer to equilibrium. Entities whose aesthetic intensity stems from the contrasts that they integrate are not guaranteed an indefinite period of existence through time. There is always the possibility that their complexity will win out over their harmony. Both triviality and confusion are capable of enduring indefinitely, but harmonized complexity is exceedingly perishable. The phenomena of life and consciousness are perhaps our best illustrations of this truth.

Permanence

Most religious and philosophical visions have intuited beyond or behind the transient flux of perishing events something or someone that preserves these events from utter loss and oblivion.[2] These visions provide consolation even in the face of perishing. The anticipation of resurrection, eternal bliss, or simply the affirmation of a transcendent, eternal God gives comfort to countless people. Tennyson's anguished lines from *In Memoriam* express the human longing for permanence in the face of perishing, and it is to such suffering as is expressed here that the religious perspectives of various peoples have been addressed:

> Oh yet we trust that somehow good
> Will be the final goal of ill,
> To pangs of nature, sins of will,
> Defects of doubt, and taints of blood;
>
> That nothing walks with aimless feet;
> That not one life shall be destroyed,
> Or cast as rubbish to the void,
> When God hath made the pile complete:
>
> That not a worm is cloven in vain;
> That not a moth with vain desire
> Is shrivelled in a fruitless fire,
> Or but subserves another's gain.
>
> Behold we know not anything;
> I can but trust that good shall fall
> At last—far off—at last, to all,
> And every winter change to spring.
>
> So runs my dream: but what am I?
> An infant crying in the night:
> An infant crying for the light:
> And with no language but a cry.
>
> O life as futile, then, as frail!
> O for thy voice to soothe and bless!

What hope of answer, or redress?
Behind the veil, behind the veil.[3]

In often quoted lines Whitehead beautifully describes the essence of the religious vision, and he does so in a manner that correlates it with Tennyson's outburst over the loss of his close friend. Religion, Whitehead says,

> ... is the vision of something which stands beyond, behind, and within, the passing flux of immediate things; something which is real, and yet waiting to be realized; something which is a remote possibility, and yet the greatest of present facts; something that gives meaning to all that passes, and yet eludes apprehension; something whose possession is the final good, and yet is beyond all reach; something which is the ultimate ideal, and the hopeless quest.[4]

And, Whitehead continues, though it "... has emerged into human experience mixed with the crudest fancies of barbaric imagination ..." nevertheless religion

> ... is our one ground for optimism. Apart from it, human life is a flash of occasional enjoyments lighting up a mass of pain and misery, a bagatelle of transient experience.[5]

Whitehead is deeply sensitive to our human experience of loss. In fact for this philosopher of process the primary metaphysical question is that of how to hold together the sense of permanence with that of perishing.[6] Is the religious vision of something that abides and that saves the world consistent with the fabric of reality as we know it from science and naive experience?

The Ground of Permanence

A contemporary of Tennyson, Arthur Hugh Clough, wrote:

It fortifies my soul to know,
That, though I perish, Truth is so.[7]

Even though every concrete thing or person is eventually lost, still its loss is not final or absolute. Charles Hartshorne explains how we may make sense of Clough's intuition:

> According to the view I adopt, there was once
> no such individual as myself, even as
> something that was "going to exist." But
> centuries after my death, there will have been
> that very individual which I am.[8]

In other words it will always and forever remain true that I have existed. Nothing can obliterate this fact. I shall die, but my perishing will not be a return to utter nothingness. Though I perish, the truth of my having existed will remain eternally.

What is there in the nature of things that guarantees that my having existed will never become a falsehood, and that I can never perish in any absolute way? Why will it be just as true two million years from now as it is today that I have lived on this earth? While I am certainly destructible, why is it that "my having existed" is indestructible? I suspect that many readers will find this kind of questioning either strange or inconsequential. But I would ask them to bear with me as I attempt to carry these peculiar probings further, and as I offer a suggestion as to how we may respond to them.

I think we must recognize that there is after all an aspect of permanence to the universe. If it is just as true today as it was a century ago that, for example, Darwin lived, then it follows that there is some kind of continuity, coherence and imperishability in the very structure of occurrences. Though Darwin has perished, the fact that Darwin once lived has not perished, nor will it ever. It is a *present* fact that Darwin lived. Hence there must be something about reality that upholds this truth and preserves it from lapsing. There is some guarantee, some rock-solid foundation to experiences that prevents their absolute annihilation after they have happened. If these experiences perished in an absolute sense we would not even be able to talk about them. They would be nothing and therefore could not be referred to. And yet we continually make reference to events, lives and experiences of the past. In some way, then, they must still be.[9]

It is not sufficient to argue, in objection to what I have just stated, that the full reality of Darwin's life and experience depends now, for whatever present existence it has, on our own thinking about or remembering it. For the very foundation of historical remembrance and historical science is that we must conform our thinking to the shape of past experiences and not superimpose our own biases and arbitrary wishes upon the past (even though this may be difficult to avoid). The ideal of historical reporting is to be as faithful to the facts of the past as possible. This ideal is based on a tacit faith that a past event's having occurred in a definite way is just as true today as it was when it happened, and that its occurrence is at least in principle accessible to our own fact-oriented inquiry today. The universe is not so capricious that it ever allows a past event to lose its character of having happened in a definite way. And for this we should be grateful.

But what is it about reality that insures the everlastingness of truth? Bergson gives us a partial clue in his analysis of duration:

> ... our duration is not merely one instant replacing another; if it were, there would never be anything but the present— no prolonging of the past into the actual, no evolution, no concrete duration. Duration is the continuous progress of the past which gnaws into the future and which swells as it advances. And as the past grows without ceasing, so also there is no limit to its preservation. .... In reality, the past is preserved by itself, automatically. In its entirety, probably, it follows us at every instant; all that we have felt, thought and willed from our earliest infancy is there, leaning over the present which is about to join it, pressing against the portals of consciousness that would fain leave it outside. .... Our past, then, as a whole, is made manifest to us in its impulse; it is felt in the form of tendency, although a small part of it only is known in the form of idea.[10]

Whitehead's philosophy expands upon Bergson's insight that all of our past experiences remain present to us and continually influence us. It shows even more explicitly than Bergson's that the preservation of the past in the present applies to the whole of cosmic reality and not merely to our own human memory. It maintains that it is of the very essence of physical reality, and not only of consciousness, that whatever has happened in the past still abides in the present. We may briefly recall how Whitehead's thought allows for this aspect of permanence within flux.

As actively feeling, inheriting and synthesizing the past, perished occasions, the actual occasions which are the ultimate constituents of the present universe preserve the past as an intrinsic aspect of their own "enjoyment." And leaving themselves open, after perishing, to being experienced by subsequent occasions, they pass on the past to their successors. We cannot overemphasize that every occasion is at root experiential. And the data that it experiences is the past. This past includes not only the immediate one, but also, in a vague sense at least, that of the entire universe. Thus nothing is ever totally lost. In perishing, the occasions of experience are not relegated to absolute nothingness but instead are assigned an "objective immortality" in the experience of subsequent occasions. The transition of things does not entail loss but preservation. In their perishing, cosmic events hand themselves over to assimilation by the present and thus are allowed to persist "immortally" as causally influential moment after moment. This objective immortality through which each event is "saved" by being deposited in the experience of subsequent events is the basis for the truth of the statement that "Darwin lived."[11]

The Loss of Immediacy

Still, our anxiety in the face of perishing will not be allayed by these cosmological considerations alone. For though we may concede the plausibility of an "objective immortality" we may still be troubled by the obvious loss of immediacy of enjoyment that characterizes all experience, ours included. Is there any sense in which such immediacy does not fade?

Whitehead himself considers this question to be perhaps the most important one that philosophy and religion have to deal with:

> The world ... is haunted by terror at the loss of the past, with its familiarities and its loved ones. It seeks escape from time in its character of 'perpetually perishing.'
>
> This is the problem which gradually shapes itself as religion reaches its higher phases in civilized communities. The most general formulation of the religious problem is the question whether the process of the temporal world passes into the formation of other actualities, bound together in an order in which novelty does not mean loss.[12]

The incursion of novelty into the world means that the present has to give way, has to perish. And this fading of the present into the past, and then the fading of the past itself is the "ultimate evil in the temporal world."[13] It is this loss of immediacy that calls forth our most anguished questioning.

> The present fact has not the past fact with it in any full immediacy. The process of time veils the past below distinctive feeling. There is a unison of becoming among things in the present. Why should there not be novelty without loss of this direct unison of immediacy among things?[14]

Paul Tillich interprets this anxiety about the loss of the present into an irretrievable past in terms of our own mortality. What makes us anxious about our having to die, he says, is not simply the possibility of our ceasing to be. Even more, it is the "anxiety of being eternally forgotten."[15] The possible fading of our memory into complete oblivion where no traces of our having existed remain is what terrorizes us. Tillich maintains that humans were never able to bear the thought of having their experience thrust into a past where it would be totally lost. And this is the reason why they have always sought in diverse ways to erect obstacles to the diminishment of their memory.

... the Greeks spoke of glory as the conquest of being forgotten. Today, the same thing is called "historical significance." If one can, one builds memorial foundations. It is consoling to think that we might be remembered for a certain time beyond death not only by those who loved us or hated us or admired us, but also by those who never knew us except now by name. Some names are remembered for centuries. Hope is expressed in the poet's proud assertion that "the traces of his earthly days cannot vanish in eons." But those traces, which unquestionably exist in the physical world, are not we ourselves, and they don't bear our name. They do not keep us from being forgotten.[16]

So perennially people have asked: "Is there anything that can keep us from being forgotten?" Is there anything that might guarantee that nothing real is ever totally pushed into the past?[17] Affirmation of purpose has always required some positive answer to these questions. Unless perishing is not absolute, unless transience is somehow compensated, it is extremely difficult to imagine how anything could be imbued with lasting significance. And unless our experience of having lived and suffered and enjoyed is somehow salvaged *in its immediacy* we will probably remain with our anxiety about death.

William James has written with deep feeling concerning the inability of a materialist philosophy of nature to prevent the complete fading of present enjoyments. Our longing for a permanence within the stream of passing events is destined for frustration if the universe is anything like that portrayed by scientific materialism:

That is the sting of it, that in the vast driftings of the cosmic weather, though many a jewelled shore appears, and many an enchanted cloud-bank floats away, long lingering ere it be dissolved—even as our world now lingers for our joy—yet when these transient products are gone, nothing, absolutely *nothing* remains, to represent those particular qualities, those elements of preciousness which they may have enshrined. Dead and gone are they, gone utterly from the very sphere and room of being. Without an echo; without a memo-

ry; without an influence on aught that may come after, to
make it care for similar ideals. This utter final wreck and
tragedy is of the essence of scientific materialism as at
present understood.[18]

God and Perishing

It is in response to this pessimism about perishing that
Whitehead's cosmological speculations turn into theological
ones.[19] He interprets the religious intuition of divine care as one
in which the immediacy of our experience is contained in God's
experience without fading, without the loss that we feel in our
own temporal perishing. The religious symbolization of such
divine care can be observed in numerous places: for example,
Jesus' belief that the very hairs of our head are numbered, that
the lilies of the field are clothed by God's grace; or the psalm-
ist's cry: "Thou hast entered my lament in thy book, my tears
are put in thy flask" (Ps 56:8). We could give countless examples of this religious intimation that somehow every experience
is salvaged and preserved eternally in its full experiential immediacy. But I think Tillich's words capture this religious optimism as well as any:

> Nothing truly real is forgotten eternally, because everything
> real comes from eternity and goes to eternity. And I speak
> now of all individual men and not solely of man. Nothing in
> the universe is unknown, nothing real is ultimately forgot-
> ten. The atom that moves in an immeasurable path today and
> the atom that moved in an immeasurable path billions of
> years ago are rooted in the eternal ground. There is no
> absolute, no completely forgotten past, because the past, like
> the future, is rooted in the divine life. Nothing is completely
> pushed into the past. Nothing real is absolutely lost and
> forgotten. We are together with everything real in the divine
> life.[20]

Whitehead's thought elaborates on the possibility of God's
preserving the past in such a way that its original immediacy of

enjoyment does not fade. There is an aspect of God's being (called God's Consequent Nature) by which God feels or experiences everything that occurs.[21] God is understood here as the ultimate recipient of all the experiences that make up the cosmic process. God retains in increasingly intense aesthetic feeling all of the vividness of immediate feeling that makes up each actual entity. God is, therefore, the feeling of all feelings, transcending the latter and gathering them together in an ever expanding pattern of beauty. Even though each momentary occasion may have lost its subjective sense of present vividness, God's own feeling preserves it in its full immediacy. Divine care also weaves into itself all of the local contradictions in cosmic experience, transforming them into a harmony of contrasts, into an unfathomable beauty. It is in this sense that the aesthetic perspective surpasses the ethical in providing a scheme for understanding divine purposiveness.

Thus God's own experience salvages what from our perspective is considered to be loss. God ". . . saves the world as it passes into the immediacy of his own experience."[22] Each experience adds a dimension of novelty and contrast and is, therefore, eternally rescued by its "relation to the completed whole."[23] It is in God's own experiential vulnerability to the cosmic process that the problem of chance in evolution also receives at least one aspect of a response. Whatever from our perspective appears to be an irremediable loss or an unintelligible deviation from cosmic order is felt by God's own feeling and transformed into contrast contributing intensity and beauty to the "wider vision." God is ". . . a tender care that nothing be lost," [24] including the vagrancy of random occurrences.

Conclusion

In God's feeling of the world the uniqueness and individuality of each aspect of reality is preserved as such. (As far as humans are concerned, there is no reason for us to reject the possibility of some sort of subjective survival beyond death as well as an objective immortality in God's own feeling.)[25] The universality of the aesthetic purposiveness of the cosmos does not diminish the value of each individual occasion by allowing it to be dissolved into the totality. The universal harmony that Dostoevski's Ivan Karamazov loathed because of its insensitivity to particular sufferings is foreign to this teleological vision (as I shall show in more detail in the following chapter). God's sensitivity to the particular feelings of every entity is unfading even while giving it a wider meaning than it can itself comprehend.

Nevertheless, the vision of God as sensitive to and preservative of all the world's experiences does not respond to an irrepressible question: granted that God empathetically embraces our joys and sufferings with everlasting immediacy, why would God allow suffering to happen in the first place? We shall now turn our attention to this issue.

10.

The Cosmic Adventure

In God's feeling of the world it is saved from perishing. The value attained by God's harmonizing the world's contrasts abides forever. The aesthetic integration of order with freshness, stability with complexity, continuity with change, form with dynamics, and unity with variety is preserved in God's experience in such a way that novelty does not mean loss after all. Instead novelty contributes to the "eternal vision" of beauty, the experience of which Whitehead refers to as Peace. It is the world's quest for this Peace, consisting in the enjoyment of Beauty, that gives it its ultimate purpose.[1]

However, God not only feels the world; the world also feels God as holding out to it an aim toward which it must strive. God in this mode of being felt by the world as the source of new possibilities is one of the things Whitehead has in mind when he talks about God's Primordial Nature.[2] Throughout the course of the preceding chapters we have been conscious of the modern scientific view that the world is a creative advance of evolution in which nature has continually experimented with new possibilities of order. These possibilities seem to be inexhaustible in their variety and depth. The arrangement of the world's occasions into an array of aggregates, organisms, and societies ranging from the subatomic to the galactic, from the simple to the complex, has no limits. The possibilities for new forms of order never seem to run out. The "whence" of these possibilities, the source of new forms of order in the world's evolution, is, in part, what we mean by God.

The world in its constituent occasions has a feel for the realm of new possibilities held out to it by God. In each moment's aesthetic "enjoyment" and "remembering" of the past it is also shaped by an influx of novelty from the transcending field of possibilities. For the most part the experiential occasions (such as those in the inorganic world) are only minimally affected by the reservoir of novelty. And so their mode of inheritance is largely one of conformity to the past, that is to say, of efficient causation. Occasionally, however, the pressure of the possible breaks through the routines of repetition and new schemes of recurrence gain a foothold in the cosmic process. Novelty insinuates itself more dramatically into the stream of becoming, allowing for the emergence of new levels of being in which there is a greater degree of sensitivity to final causation, that is, more freedom to respond to the cosmic aim of Beauty and Peace.[3]

In this sense the world is not only felt by God's aesthetic care; it also feels God as the source of new possibilities. In the mode of being felt by the world, God lures the cosmic process toward further intensification of beauty. God offers to the world, however, only those possibilities that are relevant to it at any particular phase of its becoming. For example, after the macromolecules of amino acids or nucleic acids have become sufficiently abundant, the possibility of living cells becomes a relevant new form of ordered novelty in the world's advance. But the possibility of life would not have been relevant, say, when the earth was still a seething ball of fire. Similarly, the evolution of man would have been out of place prior to the emergence of primates. In God's primordial nature there is a "grading" of the infinite variety of possibilities so that only some are applicable to each occasion's enjoyment. And even here the occasion has a "freedom" to decide which of these possibilities will be included in or excluded from its unique moment of satisfaction.

In the mode of being felt, God does not force the world to fall in line with the relevant possibilities offered to it. As we noted in Chapter 6, the world has to have an aspect of indeterminacy at every level in order for it to be a world at all.

Otherwise it would be a mere extension of God's own being. Thus the world is not compelled to pattern itself rigidly and immediately according to the shape of the relevant possibilities presented to it by God. There is room for flexibility and meandering in its response to the persuasion of its creative ground. The "principle of uncertainty" points to an indeterminacy at the level of the physical, and biology speaks of randomness at the level of life. At the conscious level the world's indeterminacy takes the form of human freedom, where persons are not compelled to follow the lure of value rooted in beauty, but may instead opt for either monotony or confusion. And at the level of civilization, we know how easy it is for the world to drift away from intense forms of ordered novelty. At all levels of the cosmic hierarchy there is at least some degree of "freedom".

Such a view of the world is not necessarily a comforting one. And it is natural for us to feel uneasy with the notion of a God who allows such a degree of "play" and "drift" to the cosmos. But I shall suggest in this chapter that the God of aesthetic care, a God of love, is also a God of adventure who does not coerce but rather persuades the world toward its fulfillment. In such a world our being ultimately cared for is not the same as a guarantee of safety. Salvation in an aesthetic scheme is not the same as being secured within a universal harmony structured according to ethical criteria. I shall approach this position by entering more explicitly into the problem of theodicy than I have done up to this point.

In the previous chapter I attempted to show how the evil of perishing is overcome by the aesthetic care of God's feeling the world and sustaining its experiences in an unfading immediacy. If God is in some way like what Whitehead calls a "fellow sufferer," however, we would still have only one aspect of a theodicy, that is, only part of a response to the "problem of evil." For just as pressing is that dimension of the theodicy problem which asks why suffering, perishing, and evil are allowed to occur in the first place. It is to this question that any reflection on the idea of God, in whatever context, eventually has to return.

The Theodicy Problem

No completely satisfying answer has yet been given to the question why, if God is a reality, powerful and benevolent, evil is allowed to exist. The question "Does not the fact of evil count against the reality of God?" will always reappear. I do not pretend that the following suggestions will adequately address this question either. For Paul Ricoeur is correct when he calls theodicy "foolishness." And yet this foolishness is irrepressible. We somehow cannot help but indulge in it.

The tremendous popularity in America of Rabbi Harold Kushner's book, *When Bad Things Happen to Good People*, is recent evidence of the perennial urgency of the theodicy question.[4] People cannot help asking why bad things are allowed to happen to them in the first place, and they understandably seek a rationally acceptable answer. I think that in many ways the "answer" Kushner gives is similar to some conclusions that may be drawn from the Whiteheadian scheme that I have outlined in the previous chapters. So it may be of some interest if I preface my discussion of theodicy by a brief summary of some of Kushner's ideas.

Rabbi Kushner states: "There is only one question which really matters: why do bad things happen to good people? All other theological conversation is intellectually diverting."[5] But in considering the alternative "solutions" that have typically been offered he finds it impossible to accept the idea of a God who deliberately wills the suffering of creatures, whether for the purpose of (1) punishment, (2) education, or (3) in order to contribute to the pattern of some "grand design." No sort of "higher purpose" can justify our individual suffering here and now.

Kushner maintains that if belief in God is to be acceptable at all, God cannot be understood as all-powerful in the sense of being able but not willing to eliminate suffering. Such an "omnipotent" God would not be capable of inspiring our love and respect. A God who could remove suffering and yet refused to do so because of its possible punitive or pedagogical value, or because it contributes to some universal plan, will only arouse our hatred. The only feasible idea of God, then, is one in which God wants to eliminate suffering but is incapable, for some reason, of doing so.

Let us explore Kushner's position by looking at the three types of theodicy he finds defective. In the first place, the idea that suffering is punishment and that we deserve what we get, instead of being an answer to the problem of theodicy, often causes even more suffering in the needless guilt that we experience when we look into our lives to dig out some hidden fault or misdeed which we suspect may have aroused God's wrath:

> The idea that God gives people what they deserve, that our misdeeds cause our misfortune, is a neat and attractive solution to the problem of evil at several levels, but it has a number of serious limitations. As we have seen, it teaches people to blame themselves. It creates guilt even where there is no basis for guilt. It makes people hate God, even as it makes them hate themselves. And most disturbing of all, it does not even fit the facts.[6]

The notion that suffering makes sense as punishment for misdeeds has a strong basis in biblical religion and in Jewish, Christian, and Islamic teaching. The main reason for its attractiveness is that it appeals to our native sense of fairness and justice. It goes hand in hand with what we earlier called the ethical vision with its demands that the universe correspond to our sense of moral order. And because of our passion for order we are willing to put up with any punishment that sustains this order.[7] The problem with this vision, however, is that it is ultimately shipwrecked, as Paul Ricoeur puts it, on the rocks of tragic suffering.[8] The story of Job, the innocent sufferer, is evidence that biblical religion itself was uncomfortable with the simplistic theodicy that makes all suffering into punishment. And Kushner's book, following a line of argument similar to that of Ricoeur, presents Job as the archetypical stumbling block to our accepting the ethical vision without qualification.

Closely associated with the theodicy of suffering as punishment is that of suffering as pedagogy. Some religious thinkers interpret our suffering as God's way of teaching us important lessons. According to this solution,

> . . . God treats us the way a wise and caring parent treats a naive child, keeping us from hurting ourselves, withholding something we may want, punishing us occasionally to make sure we understand that we have done something seriously wrong, and patiently enduring our temper tantrums at His "unfairness" in the confidence that we will one day mature and understand that it was all for our own good. "For whom the Lord loves, He chastises; even as a father does to the son he loves." (Proverbs 3:12)[9]

In this divine pedagogy God inflicts suffering on us in order to help us, and this is sufficient justification for our pain.

Kushner replies that this kind of theodicy tries to justify God, but it does nothing to alleviate concrete suffering. Kushner's objections are like those of Jürgen Moltmann, a Christian theologian, who has also clarified the flaw involved in any such theodicy. The danger is that it gives a place to suffering in the total scheme of things and thus subtly legitimates it, making us reluctant to challenge its apparent metaphysical inevitability. The bottom line of any theodicy must be the alleviation of suffering. The theodicies of punishment and pedagogy, however, do not directly attack suffering but leave the sufferer in his or her pain, rationally justifying it rather than eliminating it. Such theodicies can only drive us deeper into despair. And the God that lies behind such theodicies can only generate our resentment.[10]

A third unsatisfactory theodicy in Kushner's opinion is the one that has God causing or permitting suffering for the sake of some grand design. Perhaps my suffering is allowed or inflicted by the cosmic artist in order to add a dimension of texture and nuance to the world's canvas. My suffering is then justified by the contribution it makes to the aesthetic value of the universe. Kushner is more impressed by this aesthetic theodicy than by those of punishment and pedagogy. But he still has reservations. In the first place he thinks it might be wishful thinking since we cannot ourselves see any overall pattern of beauty. In the second place it still seems to make God monstrously insensitive to the *particular* suffering of individuals. The individual can only hate a God who sends suffering for the sake of the "grand design."[11]

Here Kushner's protest is reminiscent of that of the Russian philosopher, Nicolai Berdyaev, who like Ivan Karamazov, was repulsed by the sacrifice of the individual to any universal cosmic harmony:

> What values does the very idea of world order, world harmony possess, and could it ever in the least justify the unjust suffering of personality?
>
> . . .
>
> World harmony is a false and an enslaving idea. One must get free of it for the sake of the dignity of personality.
>
> . . .God is not world providence, that is to say not a ruler and sovereign of the universe, not *pantocrator*. God is freedom and meaning, love and sacrifice. . . . The good news of the approach of the Kingdom of God is set in opposition to the world order. It means the end of false harmony which is founded upon the realm of the common. . . . There is no need to justify, we have no right to justify, all the unhappiness, all the suffering and evil in the world with the help of the idea of God as Providence and Sovereign of the Universe.
>
> . . .
>
> God is in the child which has shed tears, and not in the world order by which those tears are said to be justified.[12]

No world order, aesthetic or otherwise, can justify the suffering of innocents. It is inexcusable that any alleged deity would sacrifice the particular for the sake of the universal.

It might seem to the reader that the present book has proposed just such a theodicy in arguing for an "aesthetic" understanding of cosmic purpose. Consequently Kushner's critique of the "grand plan" justification of God and suffering would seem to apply also to the "Whiteheadian" approach which holds that "God is the poet of the world." Hence I must address Kushner's complaints.

First Kushner maintains that we have not ourselves seen the whole cosmic tapestry and that it may be wishful thinking to suppose that there is an overall aesthetic pattern that gives a hidden answer to our suffering. Such an hypothesis, he holds, does not respond concretely to our experience of pain. In response to this objection I can only reaffirm what I stated earlier: none of us is able to have a controlling or comprehensive knowledge of any hypothetical higher level of meaning in the cosmic hierarchy or in any supposed universal pattern of beauty. If there is a universal meaning that can make sense of our particular sufferings, we cannot expect to possess such meaning. Such meaning would comprehend us rather than vice versa.

Kushner himself seems to recognize this basic religious truth as exemplified in the Book of Job which he finds to be the most important document ever written on theodicy. Job tries desperately to squeeze God into the framework of the ethical vision, seeking to measure the Almighty according to the familiar criteria of justice and moral order. But when the vision of a God who surpasses Job's narrow expectation of justice appears "out of the whirlwind," Job has to press his hands to his lips in a gesture of silence before the incomprehensible. I do not think that Kushner would deny that all genuine religious experience is characterized by such a sense of the ineffable. Therefore, the demand for clarity of comprehension in the issue of theodicy is out of place as it is in all religious consciousness. I think Kushner would agree.

Kushner's second objection to the "grand design" theodicy is more forceful, however, and we must make it a part of our own aesthetic interpretation. Like Dostoevski and Berdyaev, Kushner finds repugnant any theodicy that sacrifices the individual to the universal. I would like to express my complete sympathy with this judgment and defend the aesthetic theodicy I have adopted from any association with such a callous approach. I suspect that the source of Kushner's objections lies in the implied image or concept of God in the "grand design" type of theodicy. God is pictured or thought of as actively causing the contradictions and sufferings that give nuance and texture to the cosmic tapestry, (or if not actively causing them, at least refusing to intervene to prevent pain while having the power to do so). And it is the idea of a God who causes or deliberately tolerates evil for the sake of a higher good that justifiably arouses our sense of indignation. For this reason I am in agreement with Kushner when he points out that the real issue concerning why suffering occurs at all is that of God's power.

All three of the theodicies rejected by Kushner have in common the belief that God is the cause of our suffering, for whatever reason. And it is this belief that I would agree must be rejected. But I think it must be rejected on the very grounds of, and not in spite of, an aesthetic view of cosmic meaning. With Kushner I would be willing to say:

> Maybe God does not cause our suffering. Maybe it happens for some reason other than the will of God.
>
> . . .
>
> Could it be that God does not cause the bad things that happen to us? Could it be that He doesn't decide which families shall give birth to a handicapped child, that He did not single out Ron to be crippled by a bullet or Helen by a degenerative desease, but rather that He stands ready to help them and us cope with our tragedies if we could only get beyond the feelings of guilt and anger that separate us from Him? Could it be that "How could God do this to me?" is really the wrong question for us to ask?[13]

It is clear that for Kushner the offensiveness of the theodicies of punishment, pedagogy, and universal harmony consists in their making God the agent of suffering. Kushner is correct, I think, in focusing his critique of these theodicies on the notion of God that underlies them. He is right in maintaining that such a notion of God can only arouse our hatred. Such a God, we might add, is probably one of the major causes of modern atheism which has been highly sensitive to the "moral view of the universe," with its implied themes of order and punishment.[14]

It is because I share with Kushner (and Ricoeur) the conviction that any theodicy based on the "ethical vision" (such as those of punishment, pedagogy and universal harmony) is inadequate that I have suggested we experiment with an aesthetic vision of the cosmos. Therefore, I do not hold out the aesthetic cosmic scheme as a universal for the sake of which it is justifiable to sacrifice the individual. Instead I see the aesthetic teleological vision as one in which we may break out of the confines of the ethical criteria usually employed in theodicies that have proven to be unsatisfactory for the reasons outlined so clearly in Kushner's fine book. The aesthetic teleology I have sketched does not project some abstract universal harmony in which the suffering of individuals becomes justifiable for the sake of adding contrast to the whole cosmic tapestry. The suffering of individuals is never actively willed or desired by the ultimate source of order and novelty. What God wills, in our Whiteheadian scheme, is the fullest possible enjoyment and peace of each entity in the cosmos. The Whiteheadian view envisages God as more oriented toward the fulfillment of the individual than toward the filling out of some cosmic outline.[15] But it insists that the organismic connection of all things makes it impossible for the individual to experience fulfillment apart from the cosmos as a whole. For this reason, then, we cannot disassociate the problem of universal cosmic meaning from that of particular suffering. And so it is inevitable that our reflections on the problem of theodicy move from the individual toward the universal context of the individual's existence. And I would argue that we can more compassionately situate the concrete sufferer in an aesthetic than in an ethical universe.

In our aesthetic teleology the individual's suffering is granted a significance *in terms of* and in the context of a universal cosmic beauty. But this does not mean that the individual's suffering is justified by its potential for contributing contrast to the wider aesthetic whole. Such a view would make the "cosmic artist" monstrously insensitive, and I think we may categorically reject this idea. I would prefer to begin with the premise that the individual's suffering is never justifiable and is never actively willed or caused by God for the sake of adding beauty to the cosmic work of art. But when suffering does in fact occur (though not intrinsically justifiable) it is capable of being salvaged from sheer meaninglessness by God's aesthetic care. The individual's sufferings are felt by God with unfading sensitivity, even though they are not willed by God. God may not be capable of preventing suffering, but God is infinitely sensitive to particular sufferings, identifies with them, takes them into the divine life and transforms them into an aspect of the beauty of the cosmos in order that they never be forgotten or lost. In this way the individual's sufferings contribute to the universal without being justified by the universal.

Therefore, I can understand Berdyaev when he says that "God is in the child which has shed tears, and not in the world order by which those tears are said to be justified."[16] However, an organismic understanding of the world would prefer a different wording: "God is in the child which has shed tears, and God takes those tears into a pattern of universal beauty where they are rescued from the threat of oblivion." This at least seems to be the spirit of the Whiteheadian approach to the problem of suffering. I think that an ancient Buddhist text from the Mahayana tradition, in portraying the ideal of the bodhisattva, expresses accurately the divine sensitivity to suffering suggested by the Whiteheadian view:

> . . .it is surely better that I alone should be in pain than that all these beings should fall into the state of woe. . . . I must give myself away as a pawn through which the whole world is redeemed . . . and with this my own body I must experience, for the sake of all beings, the whole mass of all painful feelings.[17]

Only if God is something like this is the aesthetic teleology acceptable.

Adventure

I have maintained with Kushner that no overarching aesthetic teleology can justify the sufferings of individuals. But it does not follow that an aesthetic teleology cannot redeem and give meaning to individual sufferings when they do in fact occur. Nevertheless we must still ask: Why do they occur at all? Can we give any reasonable answer to this question? Kushner tells us that it may not be appropriate to ask: "How could God do this to me?" But it is certainly appropriate to ask: "What kind of God creates a world in which such things happen to me?" With the help of Whitehead and his followers, I shall propose that this God is a God of adventure and that the alternative would thrust us back into the restrictedness of the ethical vision and its correspondingly narrow, ultimately dehumanizing teleologies and theodicies.

According to modern science our universe appears to be, by all accounts, an adventure. By adventure is meant the universe's search for continually more intense forms of ordered novelty.[18] Ever since the "Big Bang" the cosmos has evolved in such a way that, little by little, more organized complexity has appeared, at least at certain points. We do not know for sure whether life or intelligent life exists elsewhere in the universe, but even if it occurs only here on earth (something which appears unlikely) we can still discern the lines of a progress toward heightened versions of ordered novelty in the cosmic advance. The living cell, for example, has an intensity of ordered complexity that elevates it far above the level of a grain of sand. And the human brain is incomparably more complex in its organization than any other state of matter of which we are aware. We can measure the progress of the cosmic adventure in terms of the criteria of harmony and complexity or of order and novelty. The criterion of adventure is the *intensity* with which the world strives to hold these contrasts together. The more adventurous the world's advance, the more possibility exists of intense syntheses of order with novelty appearing on the cosmic landscape. Because of the adventurous nature of the cosmos eventually life appeared, then consciousness, then civilization. Whatever else this cosmic adventure leads to (further expansion of consciousness? planetary unification? inter-galactic communication?) we can safely say that it would take the form of a heightening of the intensity of ordered novelty. It would continue the trend of intensifying cosmic Beauty.

If we are to speak of God at all today, then, we must correlate the idea of God with that of the cosmic adventure. Modern religious thought has not yet been able to do so in a completely satisfactory way. Whitehead and Polanyi are two of the few thinkers who have made significant strides in attempting such a correlation. They also leave many questions unanswered, but if theology is to relate itself to the facts of cosmology in the future, I think it will have to carry on the task begun by such original thinkers as these.

In the past the idea of God has been closely associated with that of cosmic order, but not often with the fact of novelty. As a result of developments in modern science we are much more aware than our theological predecessors were of the extent to which novelty continually pours into the world process. It is the fact of novelty that pulls our universe toward its adventurous experimentation with fresh forms of order in its evolution. We now must ask, more forcefully than ever before, what the idea of God has to do with the fact of novelty.

We have continually referred to God in this book as "source of order *and* novelty." But this does not make the task of theodicy any easier. For in understanding God as the source of novelty we have apparently made God responsible for the fact of evil. Let us recall that the influx of novelty into any orderly situation will inevitably disrupt that order and threaten it with the possibility of chaos. But chaos is evil; therefore, God seems to be responsible for much of what we call evil.[19]

It is tempting to revert, then, to the traditional idea that God is only source of order and to associate novelty with some other, perhaps even demonic, aspect of the universe. Much that passes as "religion" does exactly this. It refers to God as the upholder of cosmic order, an order usually framed in terms of the ethical vision, and it attributes whatever evil arises in the universe to the invasion of novelty. Such religion defends the status quo at all costs, identifies faith in God with staunch conservatism, and associates "civilized" life with stony immobility in the face of revisionist efforts.

Given the fact that innovation, especially in the area of human affairs, usually brings much immediate suffering even when its purpose is to eliminate suffering in the long run, it is easy to understand and even sympathize with the effort to associate God only with cosmic and ethical order. Revolutionaries often bring loss of life and property; visionaries are the most disturbing of all people since their entertainment of new possibilities always implies that the present order has to be overcome. So if we associate God with the realm of new possibilities we should not wonder that this God is disturbing. It might be easier to live with the God of punishment since punishment exists primarily to uphold a given order. We are willing to tolerate the idea that suffering is always the penalty for our violations of this order rather than interpret suffering as the result of the presence of novelty in the cosmic adventure. Even though biblical religion has always understood God as the source of novelty ("Behold, I make all things new"), classical theologies have predominantly associated God with cosmic order and have failed to consider in any depth the connection between God and novelty.

If we accept the world-in-process of modern science, however, we can no longer ignore the relationship of God to the novelty that renders our cosmos into an adventure. Novelty can no longer be understood as an accidental modification of order. Instead it is intrinsic to the very actuality of things. Each actual occasion is constituted by the way it feels its past. But it experiences its past (conformally or non-conformally) only in a manner shaped by its sensitivity to the new. Novelty is an aspect of each occasion. It is an essential metaphysical dimension in the process we call the universe. In fact our notion of "order" is usually the result of our abstracting from the cosmic process and freezing it into a pattern that has already dissolved and been replaced by another. "Cosmic order" can only be understood as a generalized representation of a process of successive new patternings of experience. Novelty, then, cannot be dismissed as incidental or secondary to order.[20]

Hence, we can no longer avoid thinking of God as source of novelty as well as order. God is the lure that arouses the cosmos toward adventure, constantly awakening it from the inertia that would fix it into any given order. It is because of this divine disturbance that the universe has the character of adventure which we constantly attempt to domesticate with our petty versions of ethical harmony. We find it extremely difficult to identify and coincide with the divine restlessness inherent in the cosmos. Some religious traditions, especially Buddhism, have taught that we will never find ultimate peace until we affirm this restlessness and cease our idolatrous substantializing of things and ourselves. It may take a lifetime for us to realize, as John Dunne puts it, that "...the only cure for the restlessness . . . is . . . a Yes to the restlessness itself."[21] For the most part our "religious" life seems to be most comfortable with the feeling that the present order is eternally validated. To associate religion with adventure may seem to us to be the very antithesis of what we may have taken religion to be.

Whitehead often observes how we tend to substitute a sketch for the whole picture, how we prematurely close off our openness to the cosmos and narrow ourselves down in adjusting to a mere fragment of the whole. We become fixated on a particular version of cosmic order apparently in order to avoid the evil of chaos that accompanies the urge to novelty. But in our obsession with order we succumb to monotony and triviality. Whitehead does not hesitate to call this unnecessary acquiescence in monotony an "evil" also. Evil, he says, ". . . is the brute motive force of fragmentary purpose, disregarding the eternal vision."[22] Evil, therefore, cannot be exclusively identified with chaos and perishing. It is a term applicable just as much to unnecessary triviality. Chaos and disorder constitute, of course, one form of evil. But another kind of evil belongs to those situations where a more intense harmony of novel contrasts is attainable and yet there is a reluctance to move toward a richer synthesis. "There is then the evil of triviality—a sketch in place of a full picture."[23] The aim toward beauty may be frustrated not only by the collapse into disorder as the result of too much novelty, but also by acquiescence in triviality when the appropriation of novelty is relevant. It is infidelity to the cosmic adventure to cling to low-grade forms of harmony, to remain stuck in monotony, when further advance is possible.

If the ultimate value is beauty, understood as the highest relevant synthesis of order and novelty, then it follows that too much order is just as evil as is too much novelty. Therefore, the identification of God only with order is a serious misunderstanding in our religion and theology. Such an identification is in large measure the source of the atrocities committed by humans throughout history in the name of God. The association of God only with some particular form of order has not in fact rescued God from complicity in evil any more than does the association of God with novelty.

It seems to me that it is only when God is understood as source of order *and* novelty that God is "justifiable" in terms of the problem of suffering. We could not rationally justify the existence of a God who was only the source of order since then we would wonder why the Orderer does not eliminate the disorder of suffering. Nor could we accept the idea of God as only source of novelty, since novelty without order is mere chaos. The only realistic picture of the universe we can have is one in which there is both order and chaos, one in which chaos is just as primordial as is order.[24] If we begin with this fact and keep returning to it, then we will be able to render the idea of God compatible with the cosmos after all, including its experiences of pain.

We can do so, however, only if we understand God in terms of Adventure. "God's purpose in the creative advance is the evocation of intensities."[25] God does not directly will chaos. God wills only the magnification of Beauty and the highest possible enjoyment of beauty and peace relevant to every actuality in the universe. God does not want suffering to occur, but rather wills the well-being of all things. But God does not settle for mere survival. Instead God wills the *maximum* aesthetic enjoyment relevant to each individual entity. In order for this maximum to be attainable, however, each entity must be receptive to novelty without which its present status becomes unaesthetic, unenjoyable. But in opening itself to the adventure of appropriating novelty each entity runs the risk of disintegration. Creative advance, Whitehead says, takes place only along the borders of chaos.[26] In the transition from triviality toward intensity of enjoyment there is always the risk of the evil of disorder. Evil is "the half-way house" between monotony and maximum enjoyment.[27] The cosmic adventure requires such a risk.

So it must be admitted that in maximizing the aesthetic intensity of the cosmos and of the experiences that make up the cosmos, God may be held responsible for at least some of the chaos that occurs in the cosmic process.[28] If God had not lured the process further in the direction of expanding its value (beauty), life and consciousness would never have appeared in evolution. And if life and consciousness had not appeared, then there would have been no such experience as suffering. Then we would not have any "theodicy problem." This would certainly have been one possible "solution."

Since this is not a very realistic option, however, we are still faced with the spectre of God's apparent complicity with evil in luring the cosmos to such a level of intensity that suffering becomes a possibility. John Cobb and David Griffin have approached this question by making a distinction between "responsibility" and "indictability," and at the present time I am attracted to their proposed clarification of God's relation to the fact of suffering. They insist that while God is partly responsible for much of what we call evil (meaning, I assume, that the reality of a persuasive God as source of novelty is a necessary condition of the world's creative advance), this does not mean that God is morally indictable. For it is the very "goodness" of God, manifested in a concern for maximum enjoyment for each actuality, that brings about a situation in which the evil of disorder becomes a possibility. God is not indictable for our suffering, even though were it not for God there would be no such experience as suffering in the first place. If God had not lured the cosmos toward the levels of life and consciousness nothing like suffering could have ever occurred. So in this sense God is responsible for suffering. But this does not mean that God is morally reprehensible. For God can apparently be none other than a God of Adventure.[29]

Unable to settle for the adequacy of the status quo, this God is concerned with the maximum possible fulfillment of the world and the actualities that constitute it. Our individual sufferings are never directly willed or caused by this God of Adventure. But in the world's and our own quest for beauty and peace suffering may and will occur. I doubt if we can make any sense at all of our suffering if we attempt to situate it outside of the adventurous universe of which we are a part. It is certainly difficult enough to do so even in this context, and I realize that there are many more questions raised by this chapter than I am able to respond to. Nonetheless, I think our cosmology of adventure provides a more realistic and humane setting within which to discuss the issue of theodicy than does the typical context of a fixed ethical order.

Conclusion

Why do bad things happen to good people? Rabbi Kushner suggests that there can really be no "answer." "We can offer learned explanations, but in the end, when we have covered all the squares on the game board and are feeling very proud of our cleverness, the pain and the anguish and the sense of unfairness will still be there."[30] But while there can be no answer in the form of an explanation, there may still be a "response" on our part to a world in which suffering occurs and to the God who seems to be helpless in the face of our suffering. I think Kushner has captured the spirit of the Whiteheadian approach, though his book displays no explicit familiarity with it; and so it is fitting that we end this chapter by quoting from the conclusion to his book:

> Life is not fair. The wrong people get sick and the wrong people get robbed and the wrong people get killed in wars

and accidents. Some people see life's unfairness and decide, "There is no God; the world is nothing but chaos." Others see the same unfairness and ask themselves, "Where do I get my sense of what is fair and unfair? Where do I get my sense of outrage and indignation ...? Don't I get these things from God? ... Our responding to life's unfairness with sympathy and with righteous indignation, God's compassion and God's anger working through us, may be the surest proof of all of God's reality.[31]

11.

Science and Religious Symbolism

The search for clarity has been one of the obsessions of modern thought. From Descartes through contemporary analytical philosophy the quest for lucidity in thought and language has been the dominant motif. On the surface this concern for clarity seems innocent enough. In fact it even appears noble. Any of us who are engaged in teaching require clarity of our students, and we evaluate their oral and written work accordingly. The ideal of clarity is indeed a proper aspiration of students and educators. Without clarity there can be no meaningful communication within the academic context.

However, the ideal of clarity is only a relative and not an absolute good. There are certain contexts where clarity is obtrusively out of place, and where the demand for absolute clarity is an obstacle to the growth of the mind and the promotion of life. It is a characteristic of wisdom to be able to distinguish between those areas where clarity is required and those where it would be a clumsy intruder.

The general problem of science and religion can be approached from the point of view of the question whether all knowledge and language are ideally reducible to the clear and distinct. In other words, the problem of science and religion is part of the deeper and more pervasive question whether the world in its totality can be made into a clear object to be mastered by our minds.

Because of the vague nature of the mythic-symbolic-poetic-ritualistic expressions of religion, some of those who idealize clarity find religion lacking in meaning and truth. For them truth and meaning are found only where there is clarity. Religious language, which is always symbolic, is, therefore, judged to be out of touch with the real world. According to this same contention there is no real world except that which can be mastered, comprehended or clarified by our minds, aided by science and mathematics.

The questions we have treated in this book (such as whether nature has purpose; whether biology is reducible to physics and chemistry; whether and how chance comes into play in the cosmos; and now the epistemological question of how science relates to religion) revolve around the issue of whether our universe is one-dimensional or hierarchical. A one-dimensional universe can allegedly be brought to full clarity, whereas a hierarchical universe is by definition not subject to such clarification. The term "hierarchy" may not be the best possible one to employ, nor is the term "level" entirely satisfactory. And so I have suggested that the notion of "dimension," "field" or "system" might be more apropos. Still the rules are the same: the lesser can be comprehended by but cannot comprehend the greater. If the greater is to be alluded to at all from the perspective of the lesser, the allusion will be cloudy and somewhat obscure, mastery being impossible. To an epistemology of control, however, such a situation is intolerable, and the swiftest avenue toward implementing the program of mastery is to reject out of hand the notion of a hierarchical world.

The matter of clarity vs. obscurity may also be approached from the point of view of Whitehead's philosophy of perception. I have briefly summarized it in Chapter 3, and I shall now apply it to our question of how to see scientific ideas in relation to religious symbolism.[1]

One of the most important axioms that I have found in Whitehead's thought is that those things which are most clear and distinct are not necessarily the most real. "Those elements of our experience which stand out clearly and distinctly in our consciousness are not its basic facts."[2] And, less clearly: "It must be remembered that clearness in consciousness is no evidence for primitiveness in the genetic process: the opposite doctrine is more nearly true."[3] We should indeed seek clarity, but then we should mistrust it. Why? Because clarity is the result of a process of abstracting. To abstract means to draw out (*abstraho*) certain aspects of something while leaving others behind. And it is all too easy to forget that our clear and distinct abstractions have left behind a welter of complexity. In our will to mastery we tend to set ourselves up as supreme over the abstractions we have brought forth as clear and distinct. And if mathematics is at hand we can easily slip our abstractions into the niche of the purely quantitative. Mathematics deals quite easily with the quantitatively clear and distinct, but it has trouble with the qualitatively opaque and important. In order to make things clear it has to prescind from most of what is relevant in a phenomenon, whether the latter be an atom or the universe. Whitehead's advice is to mistrust our abstractions since they are not identifiable with concrete reality. His theory of perception helps explain why.

Whitehead's Theory of Perception

"In a certain sense, everything is everywhere at all times. For every location involves an aspect of itself in every other location. Thus every spatio-temporal standpoint mirrors the world."[4] Each present moment receives the entire past set of perished occasions into its experience. Even if most of this past is only dimly felt, it is related, nonetheless, to the experience of the present moment. And it has a causal efficacy in present experience inasmuch as the present moment of experience assimilates it into its own "enjoyment."

This universal characteristic of the causal efficacy of the past in each occasion is not absent from our own experience. Our own mentality is, after all, an aspect of the cosmos. Recent scientific thinking has begun to take seriously the dramatic implications of quantum physics which posits the mutual implication of the universe and each of its constituent aspects. Hence there is no reason for us to assume that in human perception the cosmological axiom that "everything is everywhere" is suspended. Our human experience is as much tied into the structure of the cosmos as is anything else. Epistemology must correspond with cosmology. The entire universe is somehow ingredient in our own feeling as it is in every actuality. All of reality enters causally into what we have called primary perception. But the data of primary perception are not clearly delineated. They have a quality of vagueness or fuzziness about them that renders them incapable of being distinctly brought into focus. The reason for their resistance to being clearly perceived is quite simple. These data given in primary perception consist of the *whole* of reality, including its aspect of beauty, which, we have seen, is not able to be felt in its full intensity and scope from our finite perspectives. When we talk about beauty we are talking about value, purpose, aim, in other words qualities that cannot be set forth with mathematical clarity. We cannot have a controlling knowledge of the universal beauty which is the fundamental being of the universe. It is the function of symbolic expression to awaken in us a more vivid sense of the universal value (beauty, purpose) that we feel vaguely in our primary perception.

Symbolic expression is necessary to put us consciously in touch with what is the hidden metaphysical-cosmological horizon of all of our experience. And religion is perhaps the most obvious exemplification of such symbolic expression. Its purpose is to sensitize us to the ultimate value of things of which we already have a latent feeling in primary perception.

However, there is another, more immediate type of perception, that of our five senses. This secondary perception is situated at some distance from the importance we feel in primary perception. The senses present the world to our consciousness with great vividness, but in doing so they filter out much of what we gather in through our primary perception. Common sense as well as most philosophy assumes that sense perception is the fundamental way of experiencing reality. Its immediacy and lucidity seduce us into making it the criterion of knowledge. And so the empiricist orientation of modern thought (represented by Hume, Locke, Mill, and much Anglo-American philosophy) has made sense perception, aided of course by scientific instruments of observation, the basis of our understanding of the world. Because the senses present to our minds data which can be clearly and distinctly perceived and understood, we tend to assume that sense perception is the deepest and most capacious form of experience. Our senses mediate the world to us with a lucidity that is absent in primary perception. And if we are moved by the assumption that what is clear and distinct is also the most concretely real, we will be inclined to suspect the whole realm of symbolic discourse as illusory, as moving us away from rather than toward the *real* world, precisely because symbolic expression is so frustratingly nebulous. The problem of science and religion arose in the past and persists today partly because of the modern bias that the clear and distinct are also the most fundamental and that lack of clarity means absence of realism.

We may recall how Descartes gave expression to this intuition. In his obsession with discovering a sure foundation for philosophy he undertook a search for ideas that were clear and distinct. Being a mathematician he was aware that certainty, at least in that field, required the elimination of all ragged edges. The clarity and distinctness that accompany quantitative analysis became the ideal of his philosophical quest for certainty as well. And most modern thought has accompanied him both in his ideal and his quest. But since the "importance" of things is always cloaked in ambiguity the theme of value and purpose has been shoved aside as unworthy of philosophical consideration.

It is one of the most fortunate and, I suspect, controversial aspects of Whitehead's thought that it challenges both Descartes and the empiricists. Whitehead questions Descartes' assumption that "clear and distinct" necessarily means concretely real. And he chastizes the "empiricists" for not being empirical enough. His own "radical empiricism" goes deeper than the abstractions that are always the result of our attempts to clarify.[5] And this same radical empiricism strives to put us in touch with reality as it exists in its intrinsic aesthetic patterning prior to the point where our process of perception refines it down to the crisp impressions given immediately by our five senses. Radical empiricism, in other words, reaches for the world as it is always already given to us in primary perception.

A radical empiricism, therefore, lives comfortably with, even requires, symbolic expression. It recognizes (along with modern physics and religious mysticism) that our senses bite off only a tiny contemporary cross-section of reality and that our abstractive intellects may remove us even further from the intrinsic reality, depth and importance of things. It must be recalled that the intrinsic actuality of things consists in their aesthetic patterning of experience. That is to say, their reality *is* their beauty. Their reality *is* their value. Our senses can have a narrow glimpse of this intrinsic value of beauty, and our intellects can grasp a certain veneer of aesthetic patterning (especially through the use of mathematics and logic). But the past depth and present scope of reality in its comprehensive patterning and in the intensity of its intrinsic beauty can only be dimly apprehended by our sensation and abstraction. In order to compensate for this deficiency our human consciousness has searched for and has been shaped by an alternative mode of expression, the symbolic, in order to open us further to the intrinsic reality of things, namely to their importance. Radical empiricism, therefore, takes symbol seriously. This means that it takes religion seriously also.

A radical empiricism acknowledges the futility of any philosophical (or theological) attempt to reduce the intrinsic reality (beauty) of the world to ideas or impressions that can be clearly grasped. But it acknowledges that the search for clarity has a legitimate and essential role in the advance of consciousness. For this reason it does not reject the gains of modern science, empirical philosophy, or logical analysis of language. It accepts the legitimacy of certain forms of criticism and suspicion of symbols and religion. Such criticism is necessary because religious people often claim that their own symbol systems adequately represent reality. Religions fall into idolatry, which is parallel to the logical fallacy of misplaced concreteness. Our tendency to identify abstractions with concrete reality is the same tendency that moves the religious to identify their symbols with the symbolized. This human obsession with squeezing reality into containers that are not large enough needs to be challenged whether it is being done by scientists or by religious people.

A radical empiricism, therefore, can help us transcend the conflict that gives rise to most aspects of what is called the problem of science and religion. It pushes the scientific thinker beyond the illusion that the universe in its intrinsic actuality of aesthetic scope and intensity can ever be adequately grasped in the abstractions of mathematical equations. And it sensitizes religious people to the fragmentary quality of their own symbolic articulations of ultimate reality. But, in the end, a radical empiricism refuses the ideal that strives to do away with symbolism altogether. It insists on the need for art, poetry and religion to move us toward a wider and deeper conscious awareness of reality in its wider and deeper dimensions. It helps us to recognize that our symbolic life is not simply a projection of our wishes onto an insentient cosmos of primary qualities. For it teaches us first that these primary qualities are themselves abstractions from something more concrete and, second, that the aesthetic qualities which "surround" the primary qualities are intrinsic to reality itself and not mere "secondary" projections. Once we see through the logical mistakes that underlie the cosmology on which the theory of projection has parasitically fed, we can begin to locate in a fresh way just where the symbolic expression of religion fits into the structure of the evolving universe and how the language of religion relates to that of science.

The Cosmological Location of Symbolic Expression

A typical definition of symbol is "anything which, by expressing one meaning directly, expresses another indirectly."[6] Symbolic expression takes objects, persons, experiences and events that are familiar and employs them as indicators of the less familiar. A symbol, therefore, is two-sided, pointing in different directions. It has a primary intentionality whereby it stands for the familiar, and a secondary intentionality by which it draws us into the world of the unknown.[7]

The word "symbol" itself comes from the Greek *symballein*, literally, "to throw together." A symbol clasps together the two worlds of the known and the unknown. It does so in such a way that the second can be brought to awareness only by way of the first. In some way the first intention of the symbol "embodies" the second intention, and so it is intrinsically (and not arbitrarily) related to what it symbolizes.

Usually symbols are understood in what may be called a subjectivist or psychological sense. I mean that symbols are recognized as products of human imagination. The capacity of an entity to stand for another depends upon our own imagining. The use of the familiar experience of our fathers, for example, to symbolize ultimate reality (God as Father) requires our imagining the symbol's secondary intentionality. And the components of imagination differ considerably from one person to another. Because of these elements of subjectivity that characterize symbolic expression we can easily wonder whether symbols have any objective referent at all. They might be nothing more than projections without any basis in reality.

I think we have to acknowledge the susceptibility of symbols to becoming illusions. By now, however, we should be alert to the assumptions that often underlie the psychological interpretation of symbols. Above all there is the persistent bias that our mental activity is not itself part of the cosmos, and that the cosmos is an inherently valueless screen upon which we project our imagined sense of importance. I have repeatedly questioned this conviction above and I should like to do so again now with specific reference to those mental occurrences that are called symbols.

I shall propose that in addition to the psychological understanding of symbolism, where symbols seem to be no more than our imaginative creations, we must also situate symbols cosmologically. We must ask what symbols are when seen in the context of the creative advance of the universe. I shall not reject the psychological understanding, since I think we do imaginatively create our worlds symbolically and that we often do so erroneously. But I shall argue that we will seriously misinterpret our symbols unless we simultaneously view them within the more comprehensive framework of cosmology.

What, then, would be the nature of symbolic expression when defined in terms of our cosmological considerations? We may respond to this question by employing both the aesthetic and the hierarchical conceptions of the universe. (1) In the aesthetic scheme symbols "hold together" the world as it is felt in primary perception with the world as it is sensed immediately in secondary perception. (2) And in the hierarchical view symbols "hold together" the level of our human consciousness with the higher level that seeks to comprehend and integrate our consciousness (in its response of faith) into itself. Let me elaborate on each of these without giving the impression that either Whitehead or Polanyi would necessarily follow me here in my speculation.

I. Symbolism and Cosmic Beauty

In the aesthetic way of understanding the universe, the intrinsic value that resides in the whole pattern of the cosmos (most of it hidden from immediate awareness) impinges directly on our primary perception. We are affected by this value in a subliminal mode of causal feeling, and so we are usually not vividly aware of its impact upon us. Nonetheless, the ingredience of this universal aesthetic value in our primary feeling has a concrete effect upon us. It is causally efficacious in constituting us as the kind of beings we are. Concretely our being affected by this cosmic value gives us our tendency toward trust. It is in our native capacity to trust and our instinctive sense that life is worth living that we give evidence of our primordial connection to a cosmos that is intrinsically valuable.[8] Much recent research, especially in psychology, has highlighted this capacity we have for "basic trust" and has emphasized its indispensability for our personal development.[9] My conjecture here is that there are cosmological grounds for our tendency to trust consisting of the value that is inherent in the patterning of experiences that we call the universe. In our primary perception we feel ourselves linked to this universe of importance, even though clarity and distinctness are not attributes of this feeling.

Yet each of our lives is comprised of only a tiny fragment of the entire patterning which, woven together in ever newer syntheses, issues forth as our universe. Because of the narrowness and perishability of the route of occasions comprising our own lives, we command no secure vision of the universal pattern in its nuance, intensity and massiveness. Such a vision belongs only to God whose inner experience embraces the totality of cosmic experience. Consequently, owing to the restrictedness of our individual perspectives and the finiteness of our particular existence we are likely at times to shrink reality down to those aspects which we can easily abstract from or correlate with our own limited experience. And in doing this we may lose at the conscious level any sense of the intrinsic value of the whole. We may, in other words, be tempted to distrust. Distrust is possible whenever there is a weakening of the connection between the intrinsic value of reality and our own consciousness. This weakening can occur for any number of reasons, most of them having to do with the relationships we have with other persons in our immediate environment.

Even in the most extreme conditions of wounded trust, however, our causal connection with the intrinsic value of the universe is not completely severed. It is an axiom of organismic cosmology that no one is an island; even in our estrangement from others and from the cosmos (as imagined perhaps along the lines of dualism and cosmic pessimism) we are still being influenced inevitably by the totality of which we are a part. Our primary perception, which lies beyond our conscious or willful control, organically relates us to the totality, a totality that exists only inasmuch as it is patterned, a totality whose reality is, therefore, its aesthetic value. By virtue of our being part of this aesthetic whole we can never be alienated completely from its inherent value; and the fact of our being perpetually tied into it by our primary perception ensures that we can never be cut off from the metaphysical-cosmological basis of our trusting. That such a link between ourselves and cosmic value abides continuously is borne forth in our "prototypical gestures" of laughing, playing, hoping, ordering our lives, and especially in our continuing to ask questions. All of these spontaneous gestures occur only because of a fundamental trust that reality is valuable and that our lives are worth living.[10]

I have just sketched the outlines of an aesthetic cosmology indicating how each of us is tied into the cosmos through the mode of primary perception. I have reasoned (on the basis of the Whiteheadian ideas outlined in previous chapters) that we each have a subliminal feeling of the value that gives substance and actuality to the cosmic whole. But it is precisely because this feeling remains for the most part buried beneath the level of our immediate awareness that we need symbolic expression to bring this value into our conscious awareness so as to bolster and vivify our capacity to trust. We are now in a position, therefore, to specify how symbols function cosmologically.

It is through symbols, those of art, poetry and especially religion, that the intrinsic value of cosmic reality insinuates itself into the conscious experience of those organisms that we call human beings. Since these organisms are themselves creative and imaginative and are co-producers of symbols along with their fellows, their own symbolic creations add nuance, novelty and complexity to the cosmos of which they are a part. I am not entirely denying the validity of the psychological (and socio-cultural-historical) evaluation of what is involved in the fabrication of symbols, myths and stories. All I am emphasizing is that the production of symbols, like all mental occurrences, is first and foremost a cosmological event. And such an event fulfills a cosmic function. This function is to impress the value of the whole on some of the parts, specifically the human organisms, in a manner relevant to the cultural, historical and psychological situation of these organic participants in the cosmic process. Each actual occasion feels the universe's reality in a manner relevant to its experiential depth. In our human experience the reality (value) of the whole is felt at the pole of primary perception. But we also have the capacity to experience reality more clearly at the secondary pole of perception. And so our connection with the importance of things needs to be brought closer to the surface. It is the function of religious symbols in particular to bring the inherent purposefulness of the universe out of the mistiness of primary perception and into a mode of representation that can be correlated with the world of sense perception. But because the world of sense perception is too shallow to contain the depth of importance resident in the whole of reality the symbols which employ material from this shallow world (as their first intentionality) always remain somewhat off-shore in deeper waters where they appear to us only in a refracted visage. In this obscure position they "hold together" the worlds of primary and secondary perception. Symbols stand somewhere between the clear but trivial world of secondary perception and the cloudy but important world of primary perception. Given the polar nature of our perception of reality we should expect that there would be such an intermediary region of representation. And it is in this range that we find the symbolic expression of religions.

Therefore, we should not expect our religious symbols to have the clarity of scientific discourse which deals predominantly with the world that can be correlated with secondary perception. Religious symbolism strives to retrieve a universal dimension of importance that cannot be articulated with mathematical rigor. We may say, then, that religion and science are complementary modes of discourse, each related to different poles of the perceptive process. They will appear as contradictory only if we fall back into the prejudice that reduces all perception to what can be clearly grasped by the senses.

Our understanding the symbolic process in terms of the bipolar theory of perception avoids the one-sidedness of an exclusively psychological or subjectivist location of religious symbolism. It undermines the possibility of our seeing symbols as mere projections. It does so by recognizing their power and indispensability for putting us in touch with the intrinsic value (which is the reality) of things. By interpreting the symbolic process cosmologically we may envisage reality (the aesthetic whole) rather than our subjectivity as taking the initiative, first by linking us to itself in our primary perception and second by flowing through the channels of our perception until it comes closer to the pole of secondary perception (without ever quite arriving) where it can impress its importance upon us in a more vivid manner. By utilizing objects which can be correlated with sense experience symbolism mediates cosmic value to us. As reality becomes more clearly ingredient in our experience it clothes itself in those enticing and elusive configurations that we call symbols. As it moves from the vagueness of the pole of primary perception toward the crispness of the pole of secondary perception reality assumes a particularity that will appeal to our specific personal, historical and cultural experience. It does so by entrusting itself to symbols which "throw together" universality and particularity. In this sense we may appreciate symbols as revelatory of the ultimate importance (of reality) while at the same time we acknowledge our own creatively imaginative input into their production.

Anything can function as a symbol through which the depth, importance and ultimate beauty of reality discloses itself. A person, a group, an historical event, a word or a set of words, an animal, a rock, a dream etc.—any of these is capable of functioning symbolically, of mediating to us a purposefulness that transcends us and gives significance to our lives. There is no doubt that the complicity of our own imagination is a requirement of the effectiveness of these things to symbolize. But this does not mean that symbols are nothing but our imaginings. It is likely that we will be tempted toward such a reductionist position only if we have already assumed that the universe is intrinsically valueless. And it has been the main objective of the present work to challenge this assumption.

Suspicion

I think we should specify once again the cultural and philosophical background out of which the typical, psychologically biased understanding of symbols has arisen. For it is one in which most of the assumptions we have challenged in this book have reigned supreme. First it takes for granted the dichotomy of a meaning-creating subject situated over against an inherently valueless world. Accordingly symbols have been understood in modernity primarily from the point of view of the isolated epistemological subject. And this is why, in our age, there has been so much suspicion of the realism of symbolic expression. If symbols are primarily or exclusively the productions of a subject, then they probably lack objectivity. Hence they seem unrealistic.

Secondly, this psychological-subjectivist understanding of symbolism assumes the primacy of sense perception and the supremacy of clear and distinct ideas. Hence the misty world toward which symbols point and the opaqueness of this realm of ambiguity to clear logical articulation renders the symbols themselves somewhat suspect. Perhaps they are important steps toward clear understanding, but eventually they must be abandoned in the interest of a more lucid understanding of reality. More and more, symbolic expressions of all types, poetic, artistic, mythic-narrative and religious, have aroused the suspicion that they mask an underlying lack of realism, that they conceal ideological bias, fear, weakness or even hatred. And this suspicion has typically demanded that we move beyond the spuriousness of symbolism out into the clear light of daytime consciousness.

Again I would emphasize that there is a great deal of value in this suspicion. It is indeed possible for us to hide beneath our symbolism, to idolatrize it and thus to restrict our own understanding of the real world. Because of our propensity to misread our symbols we need a "hermeneutic of suspicion" to unveil our misplaced trust.[11] And yet it would be a mistake to interpret symbolism simply as a subjectivist, capricious and unnecessary mistake. The masters of suspicion are themselves part of a world that has been symbolically mediated through the myths of dualism, of tragedy or of utopian expectation. Marx, Nietzsche, Freud and their followers do not themselves recognize the degree to which their own courage of suspicion rides the tide of symbolic-mythic undercurrents in Western culture. There is little chance that we or they will ever do away with the narrative-symbolic matrices of all human consciousness and questioning.

For this reason I think we must supplement the psychological interpretation of symbolism with an interpretation that begins from the cosmos of which all acts of consciousness are a part. Once we reject the myth of dualism, we have to see all mental occurrences as part of the cosmos. Symbols, therefore, are not only subjective creations. They are that, of course, also. And creative imagination is from one point of view the source of all mythic-symbolic constructs. But from a wider point of view symbols are cosmic events which play an indispensable role in the creative advance of the universe. They are the avenues by which the principle of order and novelty lays hold of our consciousness so as to move it toward a deeper and more explicit sensitivity to value. And they are the openings made by divine care as it insinuates itself into our distrust. Symbols are two-sided phenomena. They arise from our imaginations while *at the same time* they are the result of the world's intrinsic value rising to the surface.

II. Religious Symbolism in Nature's Hierarchy

Another model of the universe has shaped our reflection throughout this book, namely, the hierarchical. How does religious symbolism fit into the emergent hierarchy of nature? Our response to this question will allow us to flesh out more fully our discussion of faith as it occurs in an emergent universe.

We have repeatedly observed that in nature's hierarchical structure the higher level dwells in and relies upon the lower but cannot be comprehended simply by an analysis of the lower. And yet, in some mode, contact is made between the higher and the lower systems, fields, dimensions or levels. In the cell, for example, there is a "holding together" of the levels of chemistry and life. It is impossible, in observing a living cell, to draw a clear line showing where chemistry stops and life begins. Vitalism attempts to posit such lines but its efforts have proven unsuccessful. I think the reason for its failure is its dualistic outlook that posits two absolutely disjunctive realms of reality, namely matter and life. Reality, as it turns out, cannot be so neatly segregated into such divergent levels. In the hierarchy of nature there are numerous junctures of assemblies and subassemblies. And in each of these there is an enfolding of the higher into the lower such that no easy disassembly is possible without destroying the phenomenon that unifies the divergent strata in the hierarchy.

At our hypothesized intersection of the level of human consciousness with that of ultimate meaning there can be no easy disentanglement of the two levels either. They are joined together in such mutual implication that one seems to melt into the other. The result of this (to us confusing) union is religious symbolism. As the level of transcendent meaning attempts to gather our human consciousness into its embrace it becomes enfleshed in forms that are familiar to us in our conscious experience. But because it is a higher level that is comprehending a lower, the symbolic forms by which it is embodied will always have a quality of incomprehensibility about them that eludes our conscious efforts at mastery. These symbolic forms will function more in the manner of drawing us into the deeper dimension than as objects which we can control intellectually. If we are comfortable with a hierarchical vision of reality we will have little difficulty in accepting the inevitable ambiguity of the symbols. But if our epistemology is one in which all of reality must lie in principle subject to our intellectual control, we will remain suspicious of all symbols. Then science will seem to be the only legitimate road to truth.

Once again, therefore, we are brought back to the question of the plausibility of a hierarchical conception of the universe. The epistemological validity of symbolic discourse requires a hierarchical conception as its necessary cosmological matrix. The legitimacy of religion in an age of science depends for its recognition on our settling for a hierarchical universe. Only in such a universe do symbols have a cosmological rather than a purely psychological status.

However, we must also acknowledge that any attraction

we may have to the hierarchical vision has itself been aroused in us by symbols themselves. Without our having been drawn toward a higher or deeper meaning by a concrete set of symbols expressed in a specific historical-cultural context we would have no inkling of ultimate purpose or of the hierarchical nature of reality. Through a specific set of narrative symbols ultimate meaning has already comprehended our consciousness and stimulated our reflection in the direction of conceiving the universe in a hierarchical fashion. "The symbol gives rise to thought."[12] In our surrender to the symbol we have already acceded to the hierarchical conception.

This may seem to involve us in a vicious circle: an appreciation of hierarchy requires an attraction to symbols which in turn draw us toward the hierarchical view. Admittedly this is a circle. Whether it is "vicious" or not, again, depends upon whether we are content with being encircled. That is, are we willing to accept that in some sense we are always comprehended by a circle of meaning that surrounds us and which we cannot get around, a circle to which we can contribute new meanings but which we cannot ourselves circumscribe? To place ourselves inside such a circle involves a risk, a "wager."[13] To imagine that our consciousness lies outside of such a circle also involves a risk. In this book I have argued that the former risk is the one more consistent with an organic universe and the cosmic adventure as it has been portrayed by modern science.

I cannot deny, therefore, that my own attraction to a hierarchical vision of reality is a consequence of my already having been taken into a specific circle of historically and culturally conditioned symbols. In my case this symbolic context is Christianity. And in the following chapter I shall sketch the relationship, as I see it, between Christian ideas of God and the aesthetic-hierarchical cosmology described above.

Conclusion

The languages of science and religion may be seen as complementary to each other. They are opposed to each other only if we make sense perception our fundamental access to reality or if we reject a hierarchical conception of the universe.

In our aesthetic model with its allied bipolar theory of perception, we can find an illuminative value in each mode of discourse, science or religion. Religious symbolism relates us especially to the intrinsic importance of reality as we feel it primordially grounding our being and becoming at the pole of primary perception. It is at this pole that all beings experience God as the silent horizon of their actuality, as the source of their intrinsic order, as the lure summoning them toward self-transcendence and, finally, as the care into which their existence is ultimately synthesized.[14] Religious symbolism represents this felt ultimacy and care by couching it in images that we may correlate with the secondary pole of perception and with our concretely limited historical experience. Because of the relative shallowness of the world as grasped in secondary perception our symbols, which borrow their first intentionality from this immediate world of sensation, are never adequate to their second intentionality. Thus they must constantly be revised in accordance with the demands of the cosmic adventure as it advances toward deeper intensity of beauty and as its freshness is deposited in primary perception. When this revision is resisted our symbols degenerate into idols which support the "evil of triviality" and which, therefore, require the criticisms we find in the likes of Marx, Nietzsche and Freud.

In this same aesthetic model we may also locate the complementary role of science. Science hovers more closely around the secondary pole of perception. This means that science deals with a much more abstract aspect of the world than does religion. Science typically disassociates its "facts" from "value." And since value, resident in the aesthetic patterning which gives actuality to all things, *is* the reality of things, any approach which neglects this value must be considered abstract rather than concrete.

Science, then, deals with "high abstractions." This observation may prove offensive to many who think that science deals more concretely with the world than does any other approach, especially religion. But our observation is not intended as a disparagement of science. There is nothing erroneous about abstractions. They are a necessary, even enriching, way of grasping the world from specific perspectives. Abstraction contributes to the advance of knowledge and civilization. The only requirement is that the abstractions be acknowledged as such. Unfortunately most modern thought has identified the concrete world with the abstractions of science and has committed the logical fallacy of misplaced concreteness. The tragedy of this fallacy is that it distracts us from any approach that would bring us back to the concrete reality of things, namely, their importance. It is the function of religion (as well as other forms of symbolic reference) to restore this concreteness to us.

Finally, the complementarity of science and religion may also be formulated in terms of our hierarchical conception. Science is a mode of knowing adequate to grasp what lies below consciousness in the hierarchy. Thus it can specify the particulars of any system in terms of the mass-energy continuum. It can legitimately employ an objectivating, comprehending and controlling epistemology. It has an indispensable function in advancing our knowledge of the universe. Religion, on the other hand, complements science by relating us to fields, dimensions or levels that lie above, or deeper than, consciousness in the cosmic hierarchy. In giving us a sense of ultimate meaning by way of its mythic-symbolic language it helps to locate us in the total "scheme of things" in a way that science, with its techniques of control, is incapable of doing. Our awareness of the hierarchical universe in all of its aspects requires our reverence of both religion and science. I shall now attempt to explain what this means for me in a Christian setting.

12.

Christianity and the Cosmos

In Christianity the primary symbol through which the ultimate meaning of the universe becomes transparent to the believer is a human personality, the man Jesus of Nazareth. It is appropriate to use the term "symbol" in referring to this man since he functions in his life and words in the manner of symbolic expression portrayed in the previous chapter. Through participation in the stories about Jesus and in the life of the community that perpetuates his memory the believer experiences a sense of being drawn into an "ultimate environment" of sustenance and care. The picture of Jesus as the Christ functions to "hold together" (sym-ballein) our immediate environment of ambiguous cosmic and interpersonal existence with an ultimate environment of unrestricted and unconditional love. For the Christian this picture functions to fortify the trust grounded in our being part of a pattern of cosmic beauty.

From the perspective of the social sciences it may appear that the symbolic power this picture has over the lives of Christians is largely a product of the intensity of the desire that gives rise to the picture as it is sketched in the New Testament and in Christian teaching and life. It may appear to be largely the believer's own wishful projections onto the gaunt life of an historical personage who in fact bore little likeness to the portrait as it exists in the imaginations of believers. It is part of our heritage in a scientific age that we would at least consider such an option as one possibility. Those of us who have been affected by the modern spirit of criticism cannot refrain from at least momentarily indulging in such suspicion. But in the present chapter I shall attempt to locate Christian symbolism in a cosmological rather than psychological context, keeping in mind our axiom that all human and mental occurrences are embedded in the cosmos. Psychology, anthropology, history, sociology, linguistics, etc., also may shed much light on the meaning and origins of Christianity. However, our perspective in this book is that of cosmology. And so, I shall devote the first part of this chapter to outlining how Christian symbolism may be situated in terms of an aesthetic cosmology and the second part to shedding light on some aspects of Christian faith in terms of the emergent-hierarchical model.

I. Christianity in an Aesthetic Perspective

The ultimate context of our lives is a pattern of ever-widening beauty lured forward, held together and felt in its massiveness and intensity by God. Our being embedded in this unfathomable totality of God and world necessarily influences us though we may have very little vivid awareness of our being so encompassed. Primary perception is the region of our being where our individual existence experiences its continuity with the totality; it is in primary perception that we feel "unconsciously" the causal influence of the aesthetic unity of God and cosmos in the constitution of our being. And so it is in primary perception that we feel the ultimate beauty and value that gives actuality to all that is. This primary organic contact with the cosmos infuses us with a subliminal sense of the world's value, and we give evidence of this primordial awareness in our tendency to trust.

However, our sense of being connected with an enlivening universe is often attenuated, and so we may also be tempted to distrust. In the state of distrust our existence becomes infected with fear, hostility, hatred, and efforts to secure our existence independently of the whole. This feeling of separation manifests itself in an obsession with what is only a fragment of the whole. It takes the attitude of acquiescence in monotony often followed by an intolerable boredom which in turn arouses within us a rage for chaos. Oscillating back and forth between monotony with its false security and chaos with its absence of limitation we either set ourselves up as omnipotent over a diminished territory or else we shrink the world into ourselves. We repress the sense of being organically encompassed by a trustworthy process infinitely larger and more important than ourselves. We lose touch somehow with reality as we feel it in primary perception.

The ultimate value that we all feel in primary perception, however, does not and cannot vanish from our primordial experience. It continues to influence us as it assimilates our lives into its ever-expanding pattern of beauty. The universal beauty which is never absent from our primary perception seeks to embody itself in symbolic forms that will evoke a response from the full range of our feelings. And so by special condensations within particular segments of reality the beauty which is reality as a whole comes to expression in particular orderings of novelty that fall within the range of our secondary awareness. Thus a flower, a sunset, a poem, a song, a person, an event or a story may become the vehicle through which total beauty makes its way from the region of global, primary perception into an area closer to our senses. As we have seen, this movement from primary to secondary perception is a process of abstraction. Much is left out in the move toward vividness. The massiveness and intensity of beauty as God experiences them cannot be felt fully in our secondary perception. So the symbolic vehicles must always be proportionate to our own concrete sense experience if they are to mediate the value of the whole to us in any way. Their particularity is both the strength and the weakness of symbols.

In Christian experience we are granted a taste of the ultimate meaning of things in the picture of a particular person's heroic life story. As was noted earlier, both genius and heroism arouse our aesthetic sense inasmuch as they are examples of the ordering of complexity into intensely dynamic patterns. The figure of Jesus as the Christ, as it is portrayed in the Gospels and as it is imitated and re-embodied in contemporary lives, has drawn numerous people into a circle of restored trust and hope. It has done so, I suspect, because it is a representation of universal beauty in a manner proportionate to a people's experience at this time in the evolution of the universe. At a time when our primordial trust has been weakened due to our experience of suffering, mortality, guilt and the threat of meaninglessness, an encounter with this picture is capable of allowing us to trust once again that we are cared for and that reality is not indifferent to our deepest longings.

In the story of Jesus the Christian is attracted to the expansiveness of the man from Nazareth who reaches out in the broadest possible way in order to integrate into his life the widest variety of people and experiences. The integration and harmonizing of contrasts is what gives his life a beauty that is compelling and healing to the believer, and that leads the Christian to understand him as the embodiment of ultimate beauty, as somehow divine. The story pictures Jesus as embracing tax collectors, prostitutes, rich and poor, the socially respected and the socially rejected, women as well as men, children and adults, heretics along with the orthodox, the sick and the healthy. He is pictured as himself a story-teller in whose stories there is equally vivid harmonizing of contrasts: a father embracing a prodigal son, a tax collector praying for forgiveness; a heretic showing a compassion far surpassing that of the orthodox, an employer rewarding laggards with the same wages as those who have worked a full day. Jesus' imagination is full of such jarring juxtapositions. And, the story goes, Jesus' own existence synthesizes the apparent contradictions of a healthy love for life with an attitude of openness to execution. It is the harmony of such sharp contrasts that summons forth our appreciation of this man. It is not finally Jesus' ethical teachings (which are not for the most part unique to him in any case) that inspire faith in him. Rather it is his relativizing of the ethical by his proclamation of a higher goodness that embraces both good and evil, the moral and the immoral. In short, it is the aesthetic dimension, the beauty portrayed in the mind and story of Jesus that calls forth a distinctively religious rather than merely ethical response from the Christian believer.

Unfortunately, though, much of Christianity has reduced Jesus to an ethical preacher. While he was certainly concerned that our life-style give expression in right behavior to our trust in God, ethics was not Jesus' primary preoccupation. Rather it was the "Reign of God," a symbol representing the Jewish hope for ultimate fulfillment and peace. This was the symbol for a time when lion would lie down with lamb, when swords would become plowshares, when the poor would possess the earth, when old men would turn to dreaming. In brief, once again, it was a symbol for the deepest possible harmony of contrasts. Jesus' prophetic vocation was to impress on people how an ultimate beauty was already breaking into their lives. He did not pretend that its appearance would be a gentle one. Instead he fully expected it to release a certain amount of chaos. And yet his hope was for a wider peace beyond the chaos. Christians today still, at times at least, share this hope.

However, to a great extent what passes as Christianity confines us to the ethical instead of opening us to the aesthetic. Sermons and religious education seem to focus more on rules of conduct than on opening our eyes to the contrasts the story of Jesus displays. Ethical concerns are an important dimension of Christian life, but they are not the ultimate horizon of faith. The ultimate horizon of faith and hope is a universal beauty. And it is our being drawn toward the spectre of eschatological beauty that gives rise to our moral aspiration in the first place. If we try to establish an ethic of duty independently of our hope for ultimate beauty, then the ethic will become an intolerable burden. The vision must precede the moral imperatives or else the imperatives will become demonic. Much contemporary atheism seems to be more aware of this fact than are many Christians.

It is partly because Christians have portrayed Jesus too dominantly in ethical terms that they leave themselves open to the suspicion of modern critics of religion. The modern rediscovery that Jesus was more preoccupied with eschatology than with morality should accordingly cause us to reassess how the figure of Jesus fits in relation to the universe. Jesus' eschatological obsession was one in which the evil in the world is not rooted out and separated from the good. Rather his vision was one in which we should allow the weeds to remain along with the wheat, one in which God allows the sun to shine on both the just and the unjust. There is no moralistic segregating of the innocent from the dark side of life. The aesthetic urge to harmonize contrasts wins out over the ethical impulse to destroy evil outright. In this attitude, then, Jesus symbolizes for the Christian the intensity and expansiveness of universal beauty that characterizes ultimate reality. He did not strive simply to tell us how to behave but, even more, to open our eyes to the wider vision. His assumption was that if we are drawn to that vision our behavior will be shaped accordingly. But he seriously objected to those who attempt to reshape our conduct in the absence of such a vision.

Therefore, Jesus insisted that the love of God for the world was comprehensive and unconditional. It embraced all contrasts in the urge for more intense unity. It is in the same spirit that subsequent Christian theological reflection has insisted that God also embraces suffering and even death as aspects of the divine life. In its teaching that God identifies with the crucified man it proclaims in effect that omnipotence empties itself and takes the form of utter weakness and helplessness. No wider or sharper contrast can be imagined than that the infinite embrace the nothingness of death. In this sense, Christian theology that focuses on the "crucified God" also presents the vision of universal beauty incipient in the teachings of and about Jesus.

No doubt it is because I am myself attracted to this vision that I have highlighted the aesthetic approach to cosmology, teleology and theodicy throughout this book. It is the image of a suffering God presented in the symbolism of Christian faith that has led me toward Whitehead's thought as an approach to cosmology which corresponds in most respects with the Christian symbolism. I would now like to show how the hierarchical model of the universe allows us further to unravel this imagery of divine vulnerability in a cosmological setting.

II. Christianity in an Emergent Universe

In the emergent hierarchy of nature each higher level dwells in and relies upon subsidiaries that constitute the lower level. For example, life dwells in and relies upon chemical processes which have to occur in a predictable and orderly manner in order for life to appear and function. This means that there is a certain "vulnerability" of the higher level in relation to a lower. Life seems to have a sort of power over the chemical level in that it is capable of integrating and organizing chemical processes into specific sequences that give it the character of life. But, at the same time, the incarnation of life in the cosmos is dependent upon the reliable performance of chemical processes. Life is fragile because of its vulnerability to being destroyed whenever there is a breakdown at the chemical level. If this vulnerability is a characteristic of all "higher" levels in their relation to the lower, then there are also theological consequences to be drawn from this condition.

The vulnerability of higher levels to malfunctions at the lower seems to intensify as we move up the ladder of emergence. Our mental processes depend for their successful achievements upon the reliable workings of biotic and physiological functions in our bodies, which in turn rely upon chemical processes. The latter in turn rely upon physical laws which themselves are orderings of quantum occurrences. The instability of entities increases as we ascend the hierarchy in the direction of human consciousness. Our conscious achievements depend for their success on an exceedingly complex hierarchy of assemblies of subassemblies. Such a ladder of ascending intensification gives an acute fragility to our humanly mental life.

Of course it is also true that a certain amount of stability is part of the very nature of hierarchies in that hierarchical structuring prevents the collapse of the whole edifice if there is a local disturbance at one of the levels. The hierarchical ordering of nature assures us that the world will not be reduced to sheer chaos every time there is a small breakdown at one level. The now famous analogy of computer scientist Herbert Simon clari-

fies this point. Huston Smith summarizes Simon's parable as
follows:

> Two watchmakers, Hora and Tempus, both make watches
> composed of a thousand parts each. Hora assembles his
> watches piece by piece, so when he drops a watch he is
> working on it falls to pieces and he must begin from scratch.
> Tempus, for his part, assembles subassemblies of ten parts
> each, joins ten of these to make a larger subassembly of a
> hundred units, and then joins ten of these to make a com-
> plete watch. If he drops a part he is working on he will have
> to repeat at most ten assembling operations and possibly
> none.[1]

Nature is structured in a manner parallel to the procedure
followed by Tempus. Consequently it is immune to the caprice
of a misplaced atom, molecule or cell here and there. Chance is
not the only factor involved in nature's emergence. Hierarchical
structuring provides the universe with a stability without which
emergence of higher levels would be impossible.

Nevertheless, there is a vulnerability of the higher to the
lower level, especially to the one immediately beneath it. We
can see this readily in the case of humanly conscious activity. If
we are physically tired we are not usually mentally alert either.
Our mental life is exceedingly vulnerable to any biological
impairment of our systems. Even though the mind has a certain
kind of power over the biological subsidiaries in which it dwells,
it is at the same time susceptible to suffering from modifications that occur within its substrata. Numerous forms of mental illness, for example, result from organic disorders in the
nervous system.

If this vulnerability of the higher to the functioning of the
lower intensifies as we move higher in the cosmic hierarchy,
then it would follow that the highest level is the most vulnerable of all. The ultimate level (field, dimension) which dwells in
and gives transcendent meaning to the whole cosmic edifice
would itself be the most precarious and susceptible to the
breakdown of the lower levels within which it dwells. God

would be open to suffering and tragedy. Is such a conclusion acceptable from a religious point of view?

I think that at least Christian symbols and reflection are congenial to this interpretation of ultimacy. (Other religious traditions are also, but I am unable to develop this suggestion here.) The image of the "crucified God" is central to Christian teaching, though perhaps it has not often been taken seriously.[2] Instead "God" has been ensconced, in classical theologies, as omnipotently immune to suffering and tragedy. The vision of the infinite emptying itself has proven to be too jarring in its contrasts for most of us. The beauty of this spectacle has been perhaps too overwhelming. And so we have typically taken the edge off of it by thinking of God primarily in ethical rather than aesthetic terms. We have subordinated the larger vision of universal beauty to the monotony of our own moral assessments of cosmic order and have invented for ourselves a God whose essential function is that of upholding our ethical orders by way of an omnipotence modeled on physical strength. Most cosmologies have been fashioned within the confines of this ethical vision and for this reason have aroused much of the modern distaste for teleology.

According to our hierarchical model, the ultimate level of meaning would also dwell in and rely upon the subsidiaries which it attempts lovingly to order into a patterning of beauty. And, if we are to be consistent, this would entail a vulnerability of the ultimate field of meaning to occurrences in the subsidiary fields. We are not required to hold that the existence of the ultimate depends upon the lesser orders. But it does seem plausible to hold that the incarnation of this ultimate in the cosmos requires an adequate preparation of its subsidiary base. Any failure at the level of the subsidiaries will impede the ingression of the divine into the world.

Of course one important level of these cosmic subsidiaries is the human. Whether this is the highest level or not we are in no position to say. But we may still conclude that in the case of God's self-embodiment in the world there is a risk of tragedy because of the precariousness of the web of human relationships that would constitute at least one of the subsidiary levels of the divine indwelling. If the actualization of our mental life is so delicately balanced on the preparation of an extremely complex physiological base, we might also maintain that the "actualization" of the divine life, on our planet at least, is even more sensitively dependent upon the preparation of a network of human relationships which would be the receptacle of the divine incarnation. In this context the Christian injunction of neighborly love (also fervently enjoined in other religious traditions) has the significance in an emergent universe of securing an interpersonal subsidiary base of sufficient order and complexity to allow for the indwelling of a divine life.

Conclusion

We cannot escape the conclusion, therefore, that our sense of divine purposefulness in the universe depends for its depth on the degree of intensity with which the human subsidiaries are tied together in a relationship of mutual love. The academic suspicion of cosmic teleology that this book has addressed and challenged has given little or no consideration to the possibility that the human level of emergence may itself become a new subsidiary in which a yet higher level (or levels) may take up residence. It seems not to have reflected deeply on the fact that by cosmic standards of chronology we are very, very early in our development as a species. Hence the prospect that "cosmic" evolution has not come to an end with the emergence of humans is something we should reflect upon seriously. We know from the past history of the cosmos that the emergence of each new level depends upon the construction of an elaborate interlacing of subsidiary components, whether these be atoms, molecules or cells. If the latest evolutionary level of units consists of persons, therefore, it behooves us to pay attention to the manner in which they cluster together and form networks of relationships. Perhaps the future of cosmic evolution depends considerably upon how communities of human individuals take shape.

Christians hold that faith in God is inseparable from the

building of true human communities bound together by a love that respects the dignity and worth of each individual. Because of this ideal, perhaps seldom realized but nevertheless kept alive somehow throughout the centuries as a compelling prospect, I cannot help agreeing with Teilhard de Chardin that Christianity has an important role to play in the future evolution of our planet.[3] As one of the religious matrices of the ideal of neighborly love and human community, but also as nurturing a hope for the coming of God climactically into the tissue of cosmic becoming, Christianity is intrinsically open to the possibility of further cosmic emergence. In fostering the necessity of human bonding in the image of the "body of Christ" or "the people of God" it promotes the preparation of a subsidiary base suitable for a deeper incarnation of God in the cosmos. For this reason it seems to me that being a Christian is an acceptable way of endorsing and fostering the scientific discoveries of modernity.

Notes

1. Huston Smith, *Beyond the Post-Modern Mind* (New York: Crossroad, 1982), pp. 83, 88; 114, 134–35.

CHAPTER 1

1. Cf. Jacques Monod, *Chance and Necessity*, trans. by. Austryn Wainhouse (New York: Vintage Books, 1972), p. 172.
2. W.T. Stace, "Man Against Darkness," *The Atlantic Monthly* CLXXXII (Sept. 1948), p. 54.
3. E.D. Klemke, "Living Without Appeal," in E.D. Klemke, ed., *The Meaning of Life* (New York: Oxford University Press, 1981), p. 169.
4. *Ibid.*, p. 170.
5. *Ibid.*, p. 172.
6. See below, Ch 7.
7. Smith, p. 114.
8. Cf. E.F. Schumacher, *A Guide for the Perplexed* (New York: Harper Colophon Books, 1977), p. 21; also Huston Smith, *Forgotten Truth* (New York: Harper Colophon Books, 1976), pp. 1–7.
9. Jacob Needleman, *A Sense of the Cosmos* (New York: E.P. Dutton Inc., Paperback Edition, 1976), pp. 10–36. The writings of Needleman, like those of Smith and Schumacher, seem to me to have at times a somewhat "gnostic" slant to them. All

three writers tend to look upon modernity as a "fall" from the pristine purity of some "primordial tradition." None of these three is able adequately to appropriate the "gains" of modern criticism and of evolutionary thought. For that reason I cannot fully endorse their positions. Nonetheless, I have been able to embrace the hierarchical mode of thinking to which they all point as the solution to the bewilderment of our scientific age. I only wish that they could have allied their hierarchical thinking more deliberately with science and evolutionary thinking. I have found in Michael Polanyi a thinker who makes this adjustment.

10. Cf. Needleman, *ibid.*

11. George Gaylord Simpson, *The Meaning of Evolution*, revised edition (New York: Bantam Books, 1971), pp. 314–15.

12. Stace, p. 54.

13. *Ibid.*

14. Paul Ricoeur, *The Symbolism of Evil*, trans. by Emerson Buchanan (Boston: Beacon Press), pp. 279ff.

15. Hywel D. Lewis, *The Elusive Self* (Philadelphia: Westminster Press, 1982), p. 1.

16. *Ibid.*, pp. 3–4.

17. *Ibid.*, p. 4.

18. *Ibid.*, p. 2.

19. *Ibid.*, p. 6.

20. Hans Jonas, *The Phenomenon of Life* (New York: Harper & Row, 1966), p. 9.

21. *Ibid.*, pp. 9–10.

22. *Ibid.*

23. Paul Tillich, *Systematic Theology*, Vol. III (Chicago: University of Chicago Press, 1963), p. 19.

24. For example, E.A. Burtt, *The Metaphysical Foundations of Modern Science* (Garden City, New York: Doubleday Anchor Books, 1954).

25. Cf. Jonas, *The Phenomenon of Life*, pp. 7–26.

26. The above six paragraphs are closely adapted from my book, *Nature and Purpose* (Lanham, Md.: University Press of America, 1980), pp. 12–14.

CHAPTER 2

1. Oparin's image is summarized by Richard H. Overman, *Evolution and the Christian Doctrine of Creation* (Philadelphia: The Westminster Press, 1967), pp. 129–30.
2. Cf. Needleman, pp. 18–20.
3. Edward O. Wilson, *On Human Nature* (New York: Bantam Books, 1979), p. 230.

CHAPTER 3

1. Alfred North Whitehead, *Science and the Modern World* (New York: The Free Press, 1967), pp. 54–55.
2. *Ibid.*, pp. 51–57; 58–59.
3. The exhortation to seek simplicity and mistrust it captures the essence of Whitehead's philosophical method and expresses the spirit of thought that runs throughout all of his writings.
4. Alfred North Whitehead, *Process and Reality*, corrected edition, ed. by David Ray Griffin and Donald W. Sherburne (New York: The Free Press, 1978); and Alfred North Whitehead, *Modes of Thought* (New York: The Free Press, 1968), pp. 86–104.
5. Henri Bergson, *Creative Evolution*, trans. by Arthur Mitchell (London: Macmillan & Company, Limited, 1911), p. 6.
6. Whitehead, *Modes of Thought*, p. 156.
7. See the fine collection of essays, *Mind in Nature*, edited by John B. Cobb, Jr. and David Ray Griffin (Lanham, Md.: University Press of America, 1977) and the less valuable symposium, *Mind in Nature*, edited by Richard Q. Elvee (San Francisco: Harper & Row, 1982).
8. David Bohm, *Wholeness and the Implicate Order* (London: Routlege and Kegan Paul, 1981), p. x.
9. *Ibid.*
10. Whitehead, *Process and Reality*, pp. 23, 25, 157ff; 221ff.
11. Cf. Charles Hartshorne, "Physics and Psychics: The Place of Mind in Nature," in Cobb and Griffin, ed., *Mind in Nature*, pp. 89–95.

12. *Ibid.*, p. 92.
13. *Ibid.*, p. 95.
14. Whitehead, *Process and Reality*, p. 190.
15. I have summarized, conflated and reformulated ideas here that may be found in numerous works of Whitehead, Hartshorne and their followers.
16. Cf., for example, Whitehead, *Process and Reality*, p. 232.
17. Cf. Hartshorne, pp. 92–93.
18. See Whitehead, *Process and Reality*, pp. 110–26; 168–83; *Modes of Thought*, pp. 148–69; and Alfred North Whitehead, *Symbolism* (New York: Capricorn Books, 1959), pp. 13–59.
19. Memory, causation and perception are all terms referring to the feeling of antecedents. "To feel (perceive) a prior event is to be causally conditioned by it, and both causation and perception are aspects of "memory"—an awareness of the past. Thus, each unit-pulsation of emotional intensity restores its antecedent universe through remembrance." Steve Odin, *Process Metaphysics and Hua-yen Buddhism* (Albany: State University of New York Press, 1982), p. 137.
20. Whitehead, *Process and Reality*, pp. 43, 47, 62.
21. Whitehead, *Modes of Thought*, p. 138.
22. *Ibid.*
23. This is Whitehead's position in *Symbolism* and elsewhere. I shall employ his theory of symbolism in a modified fashion in Chapter 11 where I shall deal directly with the question of the relationship of science to religion.

CHAPTER 4

1. Francis H.C. Crick, *Of Molecules and Men* (Seattle: University of Washington Press, 1966), p. 10.
2. J.D. Watson, *The Molecular Biology of the Gene* (New York: W.A. Benjamin, Inc., 1965), p. 67.
3. Richard Dawkins, *The Selfish Gene* (New York: Oxford University Press, 1976).
4. E.O. Wilson, *Sociobiology: The New Synthesis* (Cambridge: Belknap Press, 1975.); Ernst Mayr, "Evolution," *Scien-*

tific American CCXXXIX (Sept. 1978), p. 50; Jacques Monod, *Chance and Necessity*.

5. Monod, p. 28.

6. Quoted by John Hermann Randall, Jr., *The Making of the Modern Mind* (New York: Columbia University Press, 1976), p. 479.

7. Cf. Marjorie Grene, "The Logic of Biology," in Marjorie Grene, ed., *The Logic of Personal Knowledge* (Glencoe, Illinois: The Free Press, 1961), p. 199.

8. Cf. Ludwig von Bertalanffy, *General Systems Theory* (New York: Braziller, 1968); Ervin Laszlo, *The Systems View of the World* (New York; Braziller, 1972).

9. Wilson, *On Human Nature*, p. 2.

10. Dawkins, p. 13.

11. I am indebted here and elsewhere in this book to Michael Polanyi's *Personal Knowledge* (New York: Harper Torchbooks, 1964), esp. pp. 327–405; *The Tacit Dimension* (Garden City, New York: Doubleday Anchor Books, 1967); *Knowing and Being*, ed. by Marjorie Grene (Chicago: University of Chicago Press, 1969), pp. 225–39; and Michael Polanyi and Harry Prosch, *Meaning* (Chicago: University of Chicago Press, 1975).

12. Polanyi, *Knowing and Being*, p. 229.

13. *Ibid.*

14. The positing of such extraneous causation should not be interpreted vitalistically as a reversion to dualism. Instead it may be taken in the sense of the metaphysical principle of order and novelty that Whitehead's organismic philosophy requires (and which I shall discuss subsequently), or in the sense of formative causation (which will be introduced in the following chapter). The term "extraneous" should not be understood as "separate" or "extrinsic" but rather as "distinct" both logically and ontologically from other causal factors such as material or chemical or mechanical.

15. Marjorie Grene, "Reducibility: Another Side Issue?" in Marjorie Grene, ed., *Interpretations of Life and Mind* (New York: Humanities Press, 1971), p. 18.

CHAPTER 5

1. Polanyi, *Knowing and Being*, pp. 225–39.
2. Monod, pp. 27–28.
3. Rupert Sheldrake, *A New Science of Life* (Los Angeles: J.P. Tarcher, Inc., 1981).
4. *Ibid.*, p. 60.
5. *Ibid.*, pp. 71–91.
6. *Ibid.*, pp. 76–81.
7. Our terminology may be misleading here since according to field theory specific objects do not so much intersect with fields as perhaps *explicate*, or unfold the fields. Cf. Bohm, pp. 140–71.
8. Sheldrake, pp. 50–51.
9. *Ibid.*, pp. 12–13, 52, 59, 71, 116.
10. *Ibid.*, p. 80.
11. *Ibid.*, p. 71.
12. *Ibid.*
13. *Ibid.*, p. 95.
14. *Ibid.*
15. *Ibid.*
16. *Ibid.*, p. 96.
17. *Ibid.*, p. 97.
18. Cf. Whitehead, *Process and Reality*, p. 223.
19. Polanyi, *The Tacit Dimension*, pp. 29–52.
20. Translation by Chang Chung-yuan, *Tao: A New Way of Thinking* (New York: Harper & Row, 1975), p. 27.
21. *Ibid.*, p. 35.
22. Quoted in *ibid.*, p. 36.
23. *Ibid.*, p. 43.
24. *Ibid.*, p. 38.
25. *Ibid.*, p. 47.
26. *Ibid.*, p. 115.

CHAPTER 6

1. Monod, p. 144.
2. Cf. Bernard Lonergan, *Insight*, 3rd edition (New York: Philosophical Library, 1957), p. 114.

3. James Horigan, *Chance or Design* (New York: Philosophical Library, 1979), p. 43.

4. Monod, p. 180.

5. Cf. Whitehead, *Modes of Thought*, pp. 86–104.

6. Alfred North Whitehead, *Religion in the Making* (New York: Meridian Books, 1960), p. 115. "There is nothing actual which could be actual without some measure of order."

7. Whitehead, *Process and Reality*, pp. 32, 107, 342–51.

8. This is a central theme in both Lonergan and Whitehead.

9. Cf. Charles Birch, *Nature and God* (Philadelphia: The Westminster Press, 1965), pp. 50–80.

10. Cf. Arthur Koestler, *Janus* (New York: Random House, 1978), pp. 43ff.

CHAPTER 7

1. Cf. Schumacher, pp. 15–38; Smith, *Forgotten Truth*, pp. 1–18; 34–59; and Arthur Lovejoy, *The Great Chain of Being* (New York: Harper & Row, 1965).

2. Cf. Polanyi, *Personal Knowledge*, pp. 393–405; *The Tacit Dimension*, pp. 29–52.

3. The distinction between emergence and resultance is clarified by C. Lloyd Morgan, *Emergent Evolution* (London: William & Norgate, 1923).

4. Ernst Mayr, "Evolution," p. 50.

5. Schumacher, pp. 44–45.

6. Polanyi often uses the terms "indwelling" and "relying upon." Cf. *The Tacit Dimension*, pp. 15–18, 30, 61 and *Personal Knowledge, passim*. Again, such terms should not be interpreted dualistically or vitalistically.

7. Polanyi, *The Tacit Dimension*, pp. 35ff.

8. See Smith, *Beyond the Post-Modern Mind*, pp. 62–91.

9. *Ibid.*

10. Ricoeur, *The Symbolism of Evil*, pp. 347–57.

11. For example, B.F. Skinner, *Beyond Freedom and Dignity* (New York: Bantam Books, 1972), p. 54.

12. Smith, *Beyond the Post-Modern Mind*, p. 114.

13. I have introduced this definition of faith in *Nature and Purpose*, pp. 60ff.

14. Polanyi, *The Tacit Dimension*, pp. 40–42.

CHAPTER 8

1. Cf. Polanyi and Prosch, *Meaning*, pp. 162 and 223n.

2. Cf. Hoimar v. Ditfurth, *The Origins of Life*, trans. by Peter Heinegg (San Francisco: Harper and Row, 1982), pp. 219–36.

3. Alfred North Whitehead, *Adventures of Ideas* (New York: The Free Press, 1967), p. 265.

4. This is especially true of the works of Teilhard de Chardin.

5. Whitehead gives priority to beauty over truth and goodness in *Adventures of Ideas*, pp. 241–72.

6. Cf. William Dean, *Coming To: A Theology of Beauty* (Philadelphia: The Westminster Press, 1972).

7. See Bertrand Russell, *Religion and Science* (New York: Oxford University Press, 1961).

8. Cf. Dean Turner *Commitment to Care* (Old Greenwich, Connecticut: Devin-Adair Company, 1978).

9. Whitehead, *Adventures of Ideas*, pp. 252–96; *Process and Reality*, pp. 62, 183–85, 255 and *passim;* *Modes of Thought*, pp. 57–63. Cf. also Charles Hartshorne, *Man's Vision of God* (Chicago and New York: Willett, Clark & Company, 1941), pp. 212–29.

10. For an elaboration of this "ethical vision" see Paul Ricoeur, *The Conflict of Interpretations*, edited by Don Ihde (Evanston, Northwestern University Press, 1974), pp. 425–67.

CHAPTER 9

1. For Whitehead's discussion of "perishing" see especially *Process and Reality*, pp. 340–41; 346–51.

2. See Whitehead, *Science and the Modern World*, pp. 191–92; and Alfred North Whitehead, "Immortality," in Paul A. Schillp, ed., *The Philosophy of Alfred North Whitehead* (Evanston and Chicago: Northwestern University Press, 1941), pp. 682–700.

3. Alfred Lord Tennyson, "In Memoriam" (from Stanzas 54 and 56).

4. Whitehead, *Science and the Modern World*, pp. 191–92.

5. *Ibid.*, p. 192.

6. Whitehead, *Process and Reality*, p. 318.

7. Arthur Hugh Clough, "It Fortifies My Soul to Know."

8. Charles Hartshorne, *The Logic of Perfection* (Lasalle, Illinois: Open Court Publishing Co., 1962), p. 250.

9. Cf. *ibid.*, pp. 245–62.

10. Bergson, *Creative Evolution*, p. 5.

11. Whitehead, *Process and Reality*, pp. 29, 60, 81–82, 346–51.

12. *Ibid.*, p. 340.

13. *Ibid.*

14. *Ibid.*

15. Paul Tillich, *The Eternal Now* (New York: Charles Scribner's Sons, 1963), p. 33.

16. *Ibid.*, p. 34.

17. *Ibid.*

18. William James, *Pragmatism* (Cleveland: The World Publishing Company, Meridian Books, 1964), p. 76.

19. Whitehead, *Process and Reality*, pp. 337–51, and "Immortality," pp. 682–700.

20. Tillich, *The Eternal Now*, p. 35.

21. Whitehead, *Process and Reality*, pp. 345–51.

22. *Ibid.*, p. 346.

23. *Ibid.*

24. *Ibid.*

25. See John B. Cobb, Jr. and David Ray Griffin, *Process Theology: An Introductory Exposition* (Philadelphia: The Westminster Press, 1976), pp. 123f.

CHAPTER 10

1. Whitehead, *Adventures of Ideas*, pp. 252–96.

2. The "Primordial Nature of God" involves much more than I am bringing out here. See Whitehead, *Process and Reality*, pp. 343ff.

3. Cf. Whitehead, *Modes of Thought*, pp. 86–104; *Process and Reality*, pp. 67, 88, 349; and *Adventures of Ideas*, pp. 273–96. In this chapter I shall interpret Whitehead's ideas rather freely in terms of my own concerns with the issue of theodicy.

4. Harold S. Kushner, *When Bad Things Happen to Good People* (New York: Avon Books, 1981).

5. *Ibid.*, p. 6.

6. *Ibid.*, p. 10.

7. "Punishment only serves to preserve an already established order." Paul Ricoeur, *History and Truth*, trans. by Charles Kelbley (Evanston: Northwestern University Press, 1965), p. 125.

8. Ricoeur, *The Conflict of Interpretations*, pp. 455–67. "The critique of the god of morality finds its completion in a critique of religion as refuge and protection" (p. 456).

9. Kushner, p. 20.

10. Cf. Jürgen Moltmann, *The Trinity and the Kingdom* (San Francisco: Harper & Row, 1981), pp. 21–59.

11. Kushner, pp. 17–19.

12. Nikolai Berdyaev, *Slavery and Freedom*, trans. by R.M. French (New York: Charles Scribner's Sons, 1944), pp. 87–89, *passim*.

13. Kushner, pp. 29–30.

14. Cf. Ricoeur, *The Conflict of Interpretations*, pp 455–67.

15. Cf. Whitehead, *Process and Reality*, p. 105.

16. Berdyaev, p. 88.

17. Quoted by John Bowker, *Problems of Suffering in Religions of the World* (Cambridge: Cambridge University Press, 1970), p. 265.

18. Whitehead, *Adventures of Ideas*, pp. 258; 273–83.

19. Cobb and Griffin, pp. 69–75. Cf. also David R. Griffin, *God, Power and Evil: A Process Theodicy* (Philadelphia: Westminster Press, 1976), pp. 275–310.

20. Whitehead, *Process and Reality*, pp. 21, 28 and *passim; Modes of Thought*, pp. 85–104.

21. John Dunne, *Time and Myth* (Garden City, New York: Doubleday & Company, 1973), p. 79.

22. Whitehead, *Science and the Modern World*, p. 192.

23. Alfred North Whitehead, "Mathematics and the Good," in Schillp, ed., p. 679.

24. Cf. Clark Williamson, "Things Do Go Wrong (and Right)," *The Journal of Religion* LXIII (Jan. 1983): 44–56.

25. Whitehead, *Process and Reality*, p. 105.

26. *Ibid.*, p. 111.

27. Whitehead, *Adventures of Ideas*, p. 276.

28. Cobb and Griffin, p. 75.

29. *Ibid.*

30. Kushner, p. 147.

31. *Ibid.*, p. 142.

CHAPTER 11

1. My discussion of perception and symbolism in this chapter will appear somewhat out of focus to those readers who are pure Whiteheadians. The particular slant I have taken is nonetheless faithful, I think, to the spirit of Whitehead's thought, if not always to the letter. My discussion here is oriented only by my concern to locate religious expression in terms of science, and so for that purpose I have greatly modified Whitehead's ideas. For references see Chapter 3, n. 18.

2. Whitehead, *Process and Reality*, p. 162.

3. *Ibid.*, p. 173.

4. Whitehead, *Science and the Modern World*, p. 91.

5. Whitehead's empirical approach, like that of William James and, to some extent, George Santayana, recognizes the superficial nature of sense perception and posits a deeper, but vaguer, contact with reality. This deeper empiricism is called "radical" by James (cf. *Essays in Radical Empiricism*. New York & London: Longman, Green & Co., 1912), and Whitehead has clearly been influenced by James' "radical empiricism."

6. Cf. Ricoeur, *The Conflict of Interpretations*, pp. 12–13.

7. *Ibid.*

8. For my understanding of "trust" I am indebted to Shubert Ogden, *The Reality of God* (San Francisco: Harper &

Row, 1977); Hans Küng, *Does God Exist?* trans. by Edward Quinn (New York: Doubleday & Company, 1980), pp. 442–78; and Peter Berger, *A Rumor of Angels* (Garden City, New York: Doubleday Anchor Books, 1970), pp. 49–75.

9. Especially Erik H. Erikson, *Childhood and Society,* 2nd Editon (New York: W.W. Norton & Company, Inc., 1963), pp. 247–51.

10. Cf. Berger, pp. 49–75.

11. On the philosophy of "suspicion" see Paul Ricoeur, "The Critique of Religion," in *The Philosophy of Paul Ricoeur,* ed. by Charles E. Reagan and David Stewart (Boston: Beacon Press, 1978), p. 214.

12. Ricoeur, *The Symbolism of Evil,* p. 348.

13. *Ibid.,* pp. 355–57.

14. My Whiteheadian interpretation has also been influenced by the philosophy and theology of Karl Rahner. Cf. Karl Rahner, *Hearers of the Word,* trans. by Michael Richards (New York: Herder & Herder, 1969).

CHAPTER 12

1. Smith, *Beyond the Post-Modern Mind,* pp. 44–45.

2. Cf. Jürgen Moltmann, *The Crucified God,* trans. by R.A. Wilson and John Bowden (New York: Harper & Row, 1974).

3. Cf. Teilhard de Chardin, *The Phenomenon of Man,* trans. by Bernard Wall (New York: Harper & Row, 1959), pp. 291–98.

Index of Names

Aristotle, 77.
Asimov, Isaac, 28.
Aquinas, St. Thomas, 77.

Berdyaev, Nicolai, 125f., 129, 177n.
Berger, Peter, 179n.
Bergson, Henri, 33, 34, 112, 170n.
Bertalanffy, Ludwig von, 172n.
Birch, Charles, 174n.
Bohm, David, 36f., 170n.
Bowker, John, 177n.
Bronowski, Jacob, 28.
Buddha, 33, 34.
Burtt, E.A., 169n.

Camus, Albert, 22.
Clough, Arthur Hugh, 110, 176n.
Cobb, John, 135, 170n. 176n. 177n., 178n.
Crick, Francis, 49, 55, 171n.

Darwin, Charles, 3, 54, 55.
Dawkins, Richard, 49, 55, 171n.
Dean, William, 175n.
Democritus, 48.
Descartes, Rene, 16, 20, 48, 138, 142.
Ditfurth, Hoimar v., 175n.

Dostoevski, Fyodor, 107, 118, 126.
Dunne, John, 133, 177n.

Einstein, Albert, 79, 80, 95.
Erikson, Erik H., 179n.
Ernest Gellner, 94.

Freud, Sigmund, 151, 155.

Galileo, 15.
Gould, Stephen Jay, 28.
Grene, Marjorie, 58, 172n.
Griffin, David, 135, 170n., 176n., 177n., 178n.

Hartshorne, Charles, 38, 40, 41, 111ff., 170n., 171n., 175n., 176n.
Hegel, Georg Friedrich, 84.
Heraclitus, 33.
Horigan, James, 81, 174n.

James, William, 115, 176n., 178n.
Jastrow, Robert, 28.
Jonas, Hans, 18, 19, 169n.

Klemke, E.D., 9ff., 15, 20, 21, 22, 36, 168n.
Koestler, Arthur, 174n.

Subject Index